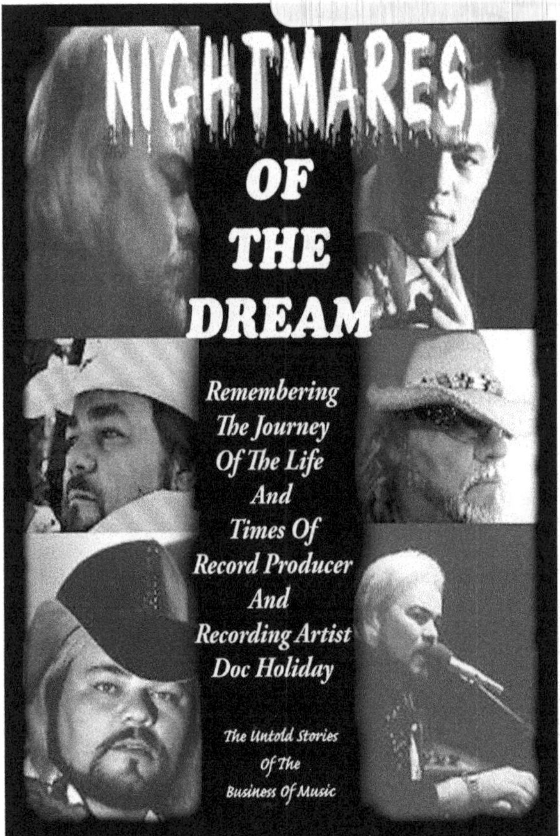

# NIGHTMARES OF THE DREAM

*Remembering The Journey Of The Life And Times Of Record Producer And Recording Artist Doc Holiday*

*The Untold Stories Of The Business Of Music*

Nightmares Of The Dream
A Musical Journey Of The Life And Time Of Doc Holiday

v3.0

The opinions expressed in this manuscript are solely the opinions of the author and do not represent the opinions or thoughts of the publisher. The author has represented and warranted full ownership and/or legal right to publish all the materials in this book.



Scattered Focus LLC

Paperback ISBN: 978-0-578-18809-6



PRINTED IN THE UNITED STATES OF AMERICA

Oh yea, and a special thanks to all the talented artists and people who came through my life that made my job so easy to do. It was you guys that made it all worth while (and you all know who you are)

And to all the haters and so-called artists that came through, that never really had the talent or skill to be there in the damn first place (and you sure as hell know who you are).

You deserve a special Thank You for forcing me to perfect my craft as a producer to make you sound good in the final product (which in most cases took some serious skills).

Remember in the entertainment business, It's not who you know, It's who knows you!!!

# Table of Contents

# In My Own Words

Hello, my name is Doc Holiday. I just celebrated (well, “celebrated” may not be the correct word) my 60th year in the “Music Business” or...Should I instead say the “Business of Music”?

I’ve achieved this anniversary as a recording artist, musician, head of a record label, touring entertainer, song publisher, songwriter, actor, radio DJ and multi-award winning record and video producer.

For many years my peers in the industry have been telling me, “Ya know Doc, ya gotta write a book and tell people about your experiences. Share those stories that went on behind the scenes in the “Music Business.” You were there!” “You seen it all happen”!, So now that I’ve reached my golden age to where my body is breaking down. My health is starting to fail and it seems time for me to actually write all this "stuff" down. I want this book to become part of my personal history. It's how I saw things that really happened in the world's craziest business called "The Music Business!" Pull up a seat...

These collected memories are not so much about my personal life, but in many instances they are, although they do touch on many parts of my career and experiences in the business of music.

My tale is about chasing that dream where I've seen so many entertainers and artists try to chase it down and become living legends. My goal is to share the hows and whys that some of those dreams had a way of turning into nightmares.

This book is about all those tales that actually happened and as to what I witnessed in my career. I'm sharing with you the reader what took place behind the scenes as well as those unspoken back room deals. The Good, The Bad and The Ugly.

It should be known that before I agreed to do this book that I made it perfectly clear to all involved that I was going to tell all of my experiences truthfully. I needed to state exactly the way that they happened. I was not pulling any punches and being brutally honest. My intention was to be allowed to name names, places, events, DJ's, promoters, executives, mobsters, and artists even though it went against my attorneys advice. However some individuals, of course, were everyday people who drifted in and out of my life because of my place and position in the business. They made an impression on me in one way or another. I'm indebted to the great artists and people that made my job of producing and performing easy and some of them I even enjoyed the challenges they created for me.

I'm also reflecting upon those few artists that were really below par in the talent department. They too took me out of my comfort zone and as a producer, I was forced to use what I knew and what studio tricks I had learned. My challenges with them was to make hit records by using my producer skills I had learned throughout the years and any tricks I mastered along the way.

You know, just think for a moment... there have been various artist which were often spoken about in recording studios behind closed doors, whose rise to success have been a mystery, because of no or very little talent. Mixing board mastery and studio tricks using modern day computers that had to be used in order to get them to sound good...and we did. It was a win win for everybody, but the unknowing public.

I sense that this book may offend, anger and upset a bunch of people because of the stories that will be told. But hey, if I'm gonna do it...I'm gonna do this the right way! My right way is to tell it all. If I can't do it that way then I'm not interested. Hell, I ain't got long to live anyway. So if you wanna come back and bitch about it, so be it. Bitch away! I'm gonna tell things the way that they were and the way they actually happened and in many cases still happen today.

My intention is to show the many times, not all, but the many incidences by which the public was manipulated and duped by the music industry. I witnessed many people first hand who went in a direction that the industry wanted them to go in order to gain the fame and fortune associated with "Stardom."

So, without further discussion, it's about time to get started here. I will begin from my earliest memory in the music industry and end with my parting thoughts upon the completed pages of this memoir. Enjoy yourself! You'll read the way so many recordings in my life really took place and as to how they continue to take place every day in this business. I already know that some of my memories may depress some people, but I also feel and hope that most of you will find my recollections interesting and helpful. You are going to see a lot of names that you will recognize and some that you may not. Every one of these individuals played a very important part in my life's story.

I must simply state one more thing before we get into my story. My daughter asked me this the other day, "Dad, if you had to do this all over again, what would you change?" I thought about it and said, "I'd do it all exactly the same way." "The only things that I would change are that I would take the booze and drugs out of my career path." "Everything else I would do exactly the same."

All these experiences that took place came together and finally fermented 60 years later. They helped to build and shape who I am and who I've become. I guess it took me a long time to figure it all out. This book may seem to get a little crazy at times, but I guess you had to be there to see what I am sharing to really fully understand it.

As I said to my friends many times, "It was always just another day in paradise." And when people have asked me when I was going to retire, my reply was simply "I'm gonna ride this bitch until the wheels fall off." Before we go any further let me leave you with this famous quote,"The music business is a cruel and shallow money trench with an insensible appetite for money. It's a long plastic hallway where thieves and pimps run free and good men die like dogs and...there's also a negative side."

"So, hold on. This is gonna be one hell of a ride!" - Doc Holiday

Oh by the way, you may see some punctuation or grammar mistakes, that's because I wrote this whole book by speaking into a recorder and I demanded that they put it down exactly that way, no corrections, These are my words!!!

# In The Beginning

Memories start to fade as I get older. They become more difficult to recall and remember. I realized if I didn't write this book now, all the secrets, events and stories would fade away.

My earliest memory where music was involved was when I was about 5 or 6 years old. My mother, Carmela or "Millie" as everybody called her, didn't want to hear anything other than I was going to be a musician, period. She used to say "Forget about being a doctor or lawyer, You are going to make your money in music". That was her dream, and it was what she instilled in me from as far back as I can remember.

She got me my first instrument at the age of 5. It was an accordion. It wasn't a small accordion, but a full adult size one. That accordion was so damn big, and I was so small you could actually see it coming close to scraping the ground while I was playing it in a picture taken of me when I was 5 or 6 years old. I was never allowed go out and play football or baseball because it was always about protecting my hands from any damage.

My mother, who nicknamed me Butchy, and was always saying, "Watch his hands!" Even as my family got into the family car my mother would say before closing the doors, "Where's his hands?" "Where's Butchy's hands?" Once everyone assured her I was in the car we went on our way. Back then all her cars were 4 door cars and I would jump in the back seat which blocked her view of where my hands were. She was terrified my hands would get slammed in the door when it closed. She was fanatical about it.

I can remember wanting to play football as a kid. There was a type of football league at the time for little kids called pop warner football. I really wanted to play bad, but my mom said, "No your gonna hurt your hands." It was the same response for little league baseball or anything else for that matter other than playing the accordion and learning music.

I grew up totally enveloped in rehearsing, practicing and learning music all the time. I had a teacher, who was a professor of music at NYU, named Eddie Kallen who came to my house twice a week for two hours at a time. I remember I would also have to practice every day for 2 hours right after school and my mom would sit there every day with me to make sure I did my exercises. By the time I finished it was time for homework and then dinner, which meant it was too late to go out and play. The only day I had off was Sunday, and that was because we went to church and finally I could hang out and play after church services. That was my whole life at that age, and that's how it was going to be, and I slowly grew to hate it.

My mother wanted me to be a musician so badly, she even named me what she thought would be a good entertainer's name. My real name is Edward, and my middle name is Martin. She felt Eddie Martin sounded like a big time entertainer, so that was that, there was no changing the name.

When I was 7 or 8 years old all the rehearsing and music lessons started to culminate and I remember my mother entering me, playing the accordion in a local talent contest. It was held at the Knights of Columbus Hall in Keyport, New Jersey. Low and behold, I won it, and the first prize was a dollar and a small trophy. That was like, "the big deal back then" A whole dollar. I got my picture and name in the local paper for winning and my mom let me keep my winnings to prove to me that we were doing the right thing, and all the hard work was worth it, and I thought "Hey maybe this stuff ain't that bad after all". After all I had won a dollar and at my age back then that was a huge score.

When I was a kid we lived in Hazlet, New Jersey on Beers Street. We had a small farm with horses, ducks chickens, you name it. I had animals all around me all the time, I guess that is why I became such an animal lover later in life. The farm was located in the country in the middle of nowhere so my only friends were the animals.

Whenever I would get a break on Sundays from practicing and getting my music lessons, I'd walk about a half a mile away down that long country road surrounded by corn fields and woods to a small little general store. It was a little country store called Johnson Brothers and they sold everything from clothes to food. They got to know me pretty well by going in there every week on Sundays with my dollar winnings and I'd walk in and say, "Can I have 5 cents worth of Swiss cheese, and a pickle please?" Back then 5 cents got you 4 or 5 thick slices of Swiss cheese, and the pickles came in a big barrel right next to the meat counter and you could pick out your own pickle and I made sure I got the biggest and best one, and that was pretty cool. Anyway, after I got my eight cents (the pickle was 3 cents) worth of cheese and a pickle, I ate it as I walked back to the farm and even broke off a few small pieces to give to the birds that were following me and an occasional rabbit that came out of the fields to get a hand out of the pickle, and by the time I got back that cheese and pickle was history.

That was my earliest memory pertaining to the business of music. I guess that's what started the whole ball rolling for me. I can say it now, that back then I didn't want to do the music stuff at all and I started to develop a real sarcastic attitude because of it. My mother made me do it and at age 5 or 6 you really didn't have much choice in the matter, But when it was all said and done I'm glad she did it. Mom was right all along. My life panned out pretty damn good in music. Like I always said "It beats the hell out of selling cars or working for a living". (Smile)

# The First Band Incident and Welcome to the Real World Kid

As the years of my youth started to fade and pass by, the increase of music in my life became more of a major part in more ways then I could ever imagine. More practice, more rehearsal, and more learning this so called art of music.

By the time I was I guess 10 or 11 years old, my mother would drag me to every Italian wedding that was being held with my accordion in hand and I would play Italian songs for the guest. It was funny because I can remember some of the reputed mobsters who I called uncle would come up at the end and point their figure at my mother after I played and say , "You, You, Millie,

Millie!" "He's got the gift." "He's got the gift!" In a way I guess it made her feel like a big deal, but ya know after a while I really got tired of playing those Italian songs at all those damn weddings. Weddings were a big deal in the Italian community in New Jersey, they went all out. So it made her proud to get their approval. I mean that's what was asked of me, and that's what I did.

But by the time I made it to the age of 13, she had gotten me an audition with a band in Lawrence Harbor, New Jersey. They were called the Harbor Lights, and I was gonna play accordion with them. They were all adults and I was around 13 or so years old. They were between the ages of 19, to 24 and their main music gigs were playing at more God damn weddings and local dances.

We played big band music from the 40s. The way I got the gig with them was I was one of the few kids around that was able to read music. It was all big band music charts. I rehearsed with them I guess for about 5 or 6 weeks at the leaders house Ted.

Remember now, I'm a 13 year old kid with all these adult musicians and I started playing those weddings and dances with them every weekend.

I can remember playing a place in Lawrence Harbor on highway 35. It was either Lawrence Harbor or Cliffwood, New Jersey which were right next to each other in central Jersey in the Raritan bay area. The place was called Burlews and it had like most places back then a huge banquet hall where they held their weekly dances and wedding receptions. We were playing Count Basie stuff, the Dorsey Brothers, Glenn Miller that kind of thing so you can probably guess what age the people were that attended.

I made like 5 or 6 bucks every time I played with them. But that was cool cause that's what they all made too. The members of the band who I can remember were the leader, Ted and he was I guess around 24 years old, one of the sax players was Jimmy from Matawan, New Jersey and the drummer was Johnny from Union Beach, New Jersey and there was a guitar player called Lootch from Elizabeth, New Jersey. There were other members of the band, but I just can't remember all of them right now.

So that night we played that dance at Burlews, and at the end of the night they said, "Hey we're gonna take a ride to Staten Island to a club there, ya wanna go?." Well I was never in Staten Island in my life. Staten Island was like the place where all the kids from Jersey went because you could drink there at 18 years old and in Jersey the drinking age was 21. I said, "Yeah cool," and I got in the car and we went to Perth Amboy, New Jersey were you caught a ferry boat for a 15 minute ride to Tottenville, Staten Island.

During that ride in the car Johnny the

drummer offered me a cigarette. I had never smoked cigarettes, but I took it just to be cool. I can remember ya know just sucking in the smoke and blowing it right out, and he said "No man, ya gotta inhale it." and he showed me how to inhale a cigarette. Well the first couple times of course like everybody else in the world I coughed my brains out and gagged, and almost passed out, not too cool right? But after a while I got used to it. I remember having 2 or 3 cigarettes within 15 mins on our way to Staten Island.

Well we crossed on the ferry boat to Staten island, and we went to a night club/bar called the Tottenville Inn. They all ordered drinks, and Johnny said, "What do you want to drink?" and I said, "Ah give me a 7up." and he went over to the bar ordered it. When he came back with the 7up I noticed it was tan colored and I said John this stuff is bad man, it's dirty, and he said no it ain't man just drink it, that's the way they do it here. I'll never forget it, the first drink I ever had in my life, a 7 and 7, Seagram 7 and & 7up. They didn't serve me. He brought it to the table like they were all drinking it and he said, "Here, go ahead. Take a drink." And I did. I drank the whole drink, and got a little woozy. So here's this night in nutshell, the first night I'm out with the band, ya know, at 13 smoking my first cigarette and drinking my first drink in a bar. I have to admit it, I kinda liked it.

But then as I look back at it today, that was in a weird kinda way my first introduction to what would become the darker side of music. Before that, it was all about the music. All about the art form. But when that happened, and I became a part of the other side of being a musician. I can remember thinking, "This is pretty cool!" I'm with these guys, and we're in Staten Island, I'm drinking, got a cigarette hanging out of my mouth and women all over the place. I don't think my mother, when she got me that job with the band realized that music had a dark side if she did she wouldn't have ever done it.

But before I knew it, I was into it and I was really liking the life style. Looking back at that point in my life I though it was getting better, but in reality it was getting worse. One of the band members was married and his wife was around 21 years old and to me she was hot!!!! I could remember thinking back going to a rehearsal and I'll be honest with you, at that time I was a virgin, I mean I talked the big talk but had not had the shot at the real deal yet. One day my mother dropped me off for a band rehearsal, but Ted had called the rehearsal off because he was working late (he did that a lot). and nobody showed up but me. I remember the house was on a hill, and it had a bunch of stairs going up to the house. It was a typical Jersey Shore house, a small cottage.

By the time I walked up those stairs my

mother had pulled away and the wife told me for some reason they forgot to call me. I said, "OK cool, but I gotta wait till my mother gets home to call her to come back and pick me up." (this was before cell phones). We lived about 40 minutes away from this place.

So I'm sitting there for 40 minutes, and the next thing I know she's offering me a drink (which I took and she was belting them down like they were Kool Aid) But I told her I can't have a 7 & 7 cause my mom smelled it on me the last time I had one and I had to tell her someone had spilled a drink on me when we played the dance, so she suggested a screwdriver, I had no idea what that was but the screw sounded pretty nice with her, she said it was made with vodka and you could not smell it.

She came over to the chair I was sitting on with the drink, I took a sip, tasted like orange juice with a little kick and she put her hand on my crotch. Ya know, I didn't know how to handle it. She was a good lookin' woman, but she was 21 years old. That's like an old lady to a 13 year old BUT A HOT OLD LADY FOR SURE. Before I knew it, she was undoing my zipper and had her face down on my lap doing what I thought was fantastic, that lead to my first experience with oral sex which lasted around 3 mins tops if I was lucky.

So she holds that memory, and that place in my history, but she also made it very clear that it was only a one time thing, She said you walked in here a kid, But I'm sending you out a man. So yup she said it was a one time thing BUT I revisited that with her for quite a while before moving on.

But it was never more than a blow job, it never progressed past that point, and I was cool with that. Like I said, unbeknownst to me my life was going down hill really damn fast. It was the other side of being a musician that I never knew existed. Nor did my mother or anyone else who was pushing me into it. But I have to admit, I was lovin it. But it kept going down hill at warped speed. So now I'm smokin', I'm drinkin', and I'm getting a BJ with a hot woman 8 years my elder (when ever her husband worked late and called off rehearsal).

Anyway, my being a part of that band continued for a few years, and it finally got to the point where I kinda outgrew the band and the music they played and thought it was moving too slow for my taste. I was also sick of playing the accordion. I remember this guy Lootch who was in the band and was the guitar player. I started talking to him about playing guitar cause in my mind I was ready to rock and the guitar was a cool instrument!!. Next thing I know, I bought myself a Fender Mustang guitar and a Fender Twin Amp. I started to teach myself and I asked Lootch to show me a couple of things, but I primarily taught myself. I fell in love with the guitar, to me it wasn't an instrument it was almost like a weapon you had on stage and could emotionally wipe out the audience.

Well, before I knew it, I formed my own first rock & roll band. I can't remember the name of the band, but there was 3 of us. There was myself and a drummer called Chickie, and I forget the other guy who was in the band, but I think he was a guitar or bass player. Anyway, we got a job at a place called the Keyport Flea Market. In the Keyport Flea Market was a teen center, and it had a stage and a little dance floor where everybody would come in on a Saturday night. I remember going out and buying a sky blue bomber jacket that made me look like James Dean with a high collar on it and I stood the collar up in the air and greased my hair back in a DA, I really thought I was the deal back then.

We were now all little juvenile delinquents or as we called it back then "Hoods", we were the cool guys (or so we thought). We played the first night and I didn't sing then. Actually nobody sang in the band, It was all instrumental stuff. I can remember the first song was called," Trouble" and it was an instrumental thing that had that twangy guitar sound that was popular back then. I think we knew 5 songs total, and I think we played the 5 songs over and over about 3 or 4 times a piece. The kids liked us. So now I'm feelin' like a rock star OK. I'm smokin', I'm drinkin', I'm getting BJ's from a hot married 21 year old Plus now I'm a rock star at the Keyport Flea Market.

We became local favorites with all the kids and started to move up in popularity locally, so of course it was time to start branching out and I booked us in a dance hall in Keansburg, New Jersey called Ballbacks. It was a dance, and it was mobbed the biggest crowd we have ever faced maybe like 200 people. It was a teen dance with kids from 12 or 13 years old to 19 years old. And that woud turn out to be my first taste of groupies in a mass quantity.

We played Ballbacks, and needless to say it went over great, they loved us, But I still had not started to sing yet, I was still just playing guitar. At the end of the night there were 7 or 8 girls that came back to the dressing rooms after the dance one was Helen, and that sport fans is when I graduated from oral sex to the whole ball game. Now, I'm really likin' music a whole lot. I'm makin' money, and I'm havin' fun. But looking back at it now, it was a huge downward slide, and it was moving faster then I knew, but I must admit I loved it. I just kept riding that wave. That band stayed together for about 2 years. By that time I was older driving a car, (with no license, a common practice back then in Jersey) and I was ready to move on and up depending on how you looked at it.

I had gotten really wild now and was a little out of control, only problem was, I didn't know it. I mean my attitude was sarcastic as hell or maybe I was starting to develop a huge ego, I thought I was 10 feet tall and bullet proof but I knew I wanted to stay in music because that's where the action was. I was kinda learning to be a bad guy now rather than being the nice little kid playing the accordion at the Italian weddings. I transitioned into a person that was extremely hard to handle and could care less what I said or who I said it too. I was not the kid my mother thought I would turn out to be. I had a lot of problems in that part of my life dealing with adulthood. But, really thinking back at it, I became an adult way before I was supposed to, and I really couldn't handle it.

# The Jersey Shore Incident

I was like hundreds of others guys my age, an impatient teen waiting on my New Jersey driver's license. During that time from when I left you in the last chapter, I got really wild, I was out of control, I'm sure you could see that coming because I sure as hell didn't.

I had a couple of serious brushes with the law. One was pretty bad. You see I was at a local Hazlet fireman fair. They had a lot of fireman's fairs around my home turf during those years to raise money because the firemen were all volunteers, and it was the Hazlet's fireman's fair that I wound up getting in a fight with a couple of military jar heads that thought they were bad just because they were in the Army. The cops were called to break up the commotion and one cop walked up to me when I was sitting in a car after kicking the shit out of the Rambo wannabes and the local cop said to me, "What's your name sunshine?" I said real smart back to him (I was wired up after the fight), "Sunshine?" "Who the fuck are you calling Sunshine jerk off?" Next thing ya know they dragged me out of the car and they had me in cuffs, and were bringing me to the police station and all the way there I was taunting the hell out of them. When I got in the police station, the front desk was up high, Ya know, it was maybe three or four feet off the ground built on a platform, and the desk was up there on the platform behind a 4 or 5 feet tall front wooden wall. I said," I get a phone call mother fuckers before you do shit." So, I called my mother. I said, "Mom, ya gotta get me outta this god damn place before I stab one of ass holes." The same cop that arrested me said, "Watch your mouth sunshine." I turned around, and had the phone in my hand. It was the old rotary type phone and I had the receiver, the talking part in my hand, and I turned around and nailed that douche bag in the face, really hard. It wound up that I broke his jaw "But I really nailed his ass", and now I got arrested for assault on a police officer and now it got really bad.

When I finally went to trial the courthouse that they tried me in was probably big enough to seat 12 people total if they were lucky. I mean it was a small out-of-the-way hic courthouse in Hazlet, New Jersey. My mother had hired court stenographers and 3 lawyers. They filled up the courthouse, nobody else could fit in. There was no room left in the courtroom and most of the cop witnesses had to wait in the hall way. It was filled with all my attorneys, stenographers, and everybody else involved in the case and of course the cops filtered in when it was their time to testify. To make a long story short, I beat the charge proving that I was antagonized and provoked by the cop.

As I was walking out, this cop that I hit who called me sunshine was standing on the porch of the courthouse, and he had his jaw all wired up from where I had broke it. My mother said, "Just get into the car, and don't say nothing." Cause I walked away with no time, no nothin', No fine. NOTHING'. I walked by him, and I remember stopping and looking right in his face. My nose was like 2 inches off his nose and I said, "Don't get old in this town mother fucker, cause I'll be there when you do, It ain't over yet Sunshine!" And I walked out. But that just goes to show you the attitude I had developed and how out of control I was. I mean, I was going crazy at that time.

And during that time, my mother kinda blamed everything on the people I was hanging around with in the music business. She suggested that I go to hair dressing school to have something to fall back on if my music career didn't take off. She enrolled me at a place in New York, in Manhattan called Atlas Beauty and Barber College. It was on the corner of 42nd street. Between 42nd and 43rd on 8th avenue. During that time I also went to Julliard School of Music (Because I had left high school and went directly to Julliard as a music protege) and was taking music classes there and I guess Julliard was around 60th street. So what I would do was, I would get on the bus in Jersey, go to the Port Authority Building in Manhattan, (that was on or around 40th St.), and walk from 40th on 8th avenue through the red light district to Julliard, do my classes there and then on the way back stop at Atlas Beauty School and do my classes there, then get on the bus and ride the bus back to Jersey which was a 2 hour ride. I guess that was her way of keeping me busy so I didn't get into any more trouble. Did it work? Yeah, for a while it worked, but I was still ready to go and raise some serious hell.

Well, before ya know it, I got my driver's license in Jersey and all hell was about to break loose. During that time I'd also been fooling around with singing and playing guitar because I never sang before and wanted to do it and just playing the guitar was not getting it done for me. I wanted more I used to go home and practice singing with Ray Charles's records. I can remember a guy in my home town that played around with music a little bit. He wasn't very good but ya know everybody played the guitar back then. Anyway, he just came up to me one day and said, "Eddie, what are you doing?" I said, "I'm practicing man." "To sound like Ray Charles". He said, "Hey man stop that shit, you do Eddie better than anybody else!" And that was where reality first set in, right then and there. I mean that's the moment where the light bulb went off in my head, He was right!" I started working on singing my way, with my own voice instead of trying sound like Ray Charles.

Well, my life went on and the music was still a major part of it, BUT I was keeping this tremendous schedule up between Julliard and Beauty School.

I graduated beauty school, and got a job in Lincroft, New Jersey at a place called Franks Lincroff Barber shop owned by a guy named Frank Cordasco. While I was working there, one of the customers came in. His name was Chuck, I remember thinking, what a jerk off, a little rich kid ass hole" Lincroft was considered to be somewhat of a rich type area, with big houses, and big race horse farms. Chucks parents owned a big horse farm in Colts Neck a little town right next to Lincroft. Back then, that was the big high class area of Jersey. During that time my parents had moved from that small farm in Hazlet we lived at and my mother built a huge house in Homdel, New Jersey on 12 acres of land. Homdel was like the Beverly Hills of New Jersey and it still is today. She built a huge house with a three car garage, a horseshoe driveway, and she actually put an in ground swimming pool behind the house. Back then we were the only one in a 50 mile radius that had an in ground swimming pool.

So, my parents were doing really well. My father was getting high up in the teamsters union along with Jimmy Hoffa. BUT I was still the maniac wild one in the family. But, my mother, I gotta give her credit, she stuck with me no matter what I did and what ever trouble I managed to get in, she never gave up on me and she went the whole nine yards to make every wrong right.

OK getting back to Chuck. Chuck had mentioned to me when he was in the shop getting a hair cut that he played bass in a band, and he knew I was interested and passionate about being in music, and invited me up that weekend to see the band in Belmar, New Jersey a small seaside town on the Jersey shore, and I went up there one night to check them out.

The name of their band was The Fidells and it was a four piece band, kind of a typical Jersey shore bar band. The members were Mike DeStefano on guitar, Don Scacia on drums, Jerry Benicasa on Sax and of course Chuck on bass. They covered a lot of rock and roll music from the

50's and very early 60's. The guitar player, Mike, was the only real singer in the band, nobody else sang but Mike handled it really good. I went up there one night by myself and they asked me to set in and sing and play guitar on a few tunes, and they liked what I was doing and the way I played and sang, and the best of all I saw potential in what they were doing. So somehow we got together and talked to like 5am that night, and I went over to Chucks house a few nights later and we started to rehearse.

I immediately said, "Listen, we gotta change the name of this band." "This name "The Fidells) really sucked and didn't represent the sound and material we were now putting out. It was kinda a bold move on my part since I had just started with the band. So with some serious prodding by me we all agreed on a name the Ducanes. Me & Mike suggested that we would take a band picture wearing black stove pipe top hats, canes, ascots, Black blazers, and of course high heel Beatle Boots, Ya see band pictures were a must back then, all of the bands had them at that time, we all agreed to fork up the money get the pictures professionally done. And the next thing I said, "Listen, the sax player has got to go." "Ya know, we don't need a sax player because the English sound was coming in, and the sound was all guitar driven, and it didn't need a sax plus as I can remember he wasn't that good to begin with."

So the final band was, Mike, myself, Donald, and Chuck and we started working our asses off perfecting a sound that was a blend of 50's Do Wop oldies blended with soul music (That's what R&B was called back then) and threw in some of the British band sound that were really becoming popular then.

We started rehearsing at Chuck's house 8 to 10 hours every night, 7 nights a week, and got Chuck (I should say me & Mike forced him) to start singing harmony/back up singing and you could start to see the magic starting to happen. We were pushing the envelope to create new sounds and arrangements. Well before you know it, it was time to take the band out and start performing for the public. The first job that we landed after 8 weeks of rehearsing was at a place called The Polka Dot Lounge in Long Branch, New Jersey. The band was really starting to come together now and Mike had a great voice, he was probably the most talented of the group other than myself of course (smile). Mike and me were trading off singing and Mike would do a lot of the harmony parts when I was singing lead. And I actually got (I mean forced) Donald to sing a few songs. He did some comedic type songs that did not require a great voice.

Well we played at the Polka Dot for about 6 months, and we blew it apart. I mean we were the hottest thing since sliced bread in there, and we just kept jamming it with huge crowds. So now, we're on our way. However, the other guys in the band didn't have the passion that I had. Ya know, this was gonna be my future and I wanted more. This was what I wanted, and this band was nothing more than the stepping stone to get to where I needed to be. They, on the other hand, all had day jobs that they were into. The band was like a hobby to them, but not to me. It was a weekend warrior thing with them. But like I said, in my mind, I was going for the brass ring with it.

Moving along from there we started to play other clubs in and around the shore area and every club we played at we just blew apart, we had a huge following and our reputation was growing fast (maybe a little too fast for us to handle). I mean we leveled every club we performed in. It was unbelievable. People waiting in lines to get in. It was unreal, the money, the woman, and everything that went along with being a hot local band was an every night thing. That went on for awhile but I wanted more than playing weekends in clubs, but I knew just playing weekends was not gonna get me where I needed to be plus we did not have the endurance we needed to really click as a top band. By that I mean we needed to play more than two nights a week, so I booked us into a club in Belmar called "The Surf Club", 6 nights a week plus a matinee on Saturday afternoons. Now that was a grind for all of us, Plus I was still working at the shop in Lincroft 6 days a week. So in short I would go to work at the shop at 9am till 6pm, rush home clean up, grab a bite to eat, and then drive an hour to Belmar, perform until 2am, party with the groupies until like 4am, drive back home grab 3 hours of sleep and do it all over again 6 days and nights a week. OK now I proved to myself I had the staying power on stage to get it done. But it also introduced a thing called "Black Beauty's" or in short "SPEED, Meth as it is known in today's world. I use to called them pocket rockets and they kept me going BUT the black beauties were also setting me up for the horror of what I would become.

DeStefano was a great guitar player, plus he had a great look, the woman loved that pretty boy face. I got him into doing some songwriting with me cause like I said I wanted more and I knew I had to start to create a special sound and songs that were totally different from the other stuff that we were playing in the clubs.

We decided during that time period to take a shot at going into a recording studio and do some of our original material that me and Mike had written. This was actually the first really big studio I had ever been in. It was the RCA studios in Camden, New Jersey. We all went in, and we recorded 3 songs. They came out pretty damn good. Matter of fact, you can still hear some of them around the internet. Me and Mike wrote two originals out of the 3 we cut and we both sang them with me on the lead and Mike doing the harmony, and it really came out better than anyone expected, actually it came out pretty damn awesome if I do say so.

But that night being in a real recording studio gave me the taste for where I needed to be in this business, I said OK, this is what I wanna do, this is where I had to be when it was all said and done. I wanna be in a studio creating. I don't wanna be in a fuckin' bar. I don't wanna be doin' this shit until 2 in the morning surrounded by a bunch of fuckin' drunks that were more concerned with the girls we were drawing in every night then the music we were doing. I wanted be in a recording studio creating that next big sound, I hated playing cover songs in bars. My goal now had changed and changed quick, but I needed to work in this band to experiment with new songs and sounds to get where I had the shot to move to where I needed to be in the business BUT slowly the drugs I was taking were starting to little by little take control of me.

We got a major shot to do a show at a place called, The Ocean Ice Palace in Bricktown, New Jersey. The place held like 2000 people if it was sold out . The show featured a local group called "THE JERSEY BEATLES" that in my opinion sucked big time. I mean they were terrible and we were set to open for an act called the Dixie Cups who at the time had the number one record in the country "Going to the Chapel of Love." So while the guys were like enjoying the fans and groupies out front, I got with the manger of the Dixie Cups back stage, and started to pick his brain, and figure out how they got to where they were with a # 1 record and tried to figure out the business end of it and how it all worked. So we went on that night and opened for The Dixie Cups, and we totally destroyed the place. I mean we were that good. We were a hot ass band on the Jersey shore at that time, and like I said, Mike on the guitar was awesome. Donald on drums, I mean he was as solid as a rock. Once he set the beat, that was it. It wasn't movin'. Ya know he kicked our ass's with that grove, Chuck, ah man, he had his fingers up his ass as usual. I don't know what the hell he was doin'? He was playing his four notes doing whatever he did and lookin' like a nit wit doing it. So that show would turn out to be a high note for us, we were all 10 feet tall and bullet proof that night.

Anyway after that job, like I said, I was focused on getting back into the studio and making a hit record. So it got to a point right after that where I just said I gotta move on, and Mike had some personal issues going on and the band broke up and I moved on.

However when I left the band, I got a call from a guy called, Stormin Norman Seldin.

Norman was probably the biggest unsung hero on the Jersey Shore during that time. He was a keyboard player. He was a young guy, like only 17 or 18 years old and was tremendous on the piano, I mean make no mistake about it he could play his ass off, Plus he was a promoter on top of it all. At 17 years old this guy was promoting huge concerts. He had called me and wanted to start a band called, The Soul Set. The term "Soul" was the label they put on black music back then and Norman wanted a white band that could sound black and it just so happened, that my voice fit that sound to a tee. So I joined up with him.

It was myself and Norman and he said we need a drummer so I called Donald from the Ducanes because like I said earlier he was solid as a rock and could play that shit like no other white boy could. I figured because I was a lot older than Norman it may poise a problem, but it did not, we locked in like brothers.

I said, "Donald, ya wanna play with us man we're gonna do this soul thing?" And Don said, "Sure." So it was me, Donald, and Norman, a power trio. We didn't need a bass player because Norman was so strong with his left hand that he played the bass parts with his left hand while doing the piano and organ parts with his right hand plus I forgot to mention Norman also sang his ass off doing it all at the same time (Norman had his shit together). This was a big move for me because Norman was playing all these big concert dates with major acts and I needed to get that exposure at that level of the business.

The first show we did with Norman was at the Matawan roller rink in Matawan, New Jersey and we opened for the Rascals, they had the number one record in the country at the time. Norman suggested we all buy long hair wigs and wear them on stage to give us a better look, since we all had fairly short hair and long hair was coming into style back then with the advent of the Beatles. The only problem was when we were on stage performing our set Donald's wig flew off his head while we were playing and landed on the floor behind him, BUT no one, thank God noticed because the drummer was set up behind me and Norman and it was the last song of the set.

So now we're facing huge crowds with major recording artists, right where I needed to be. That night there was also a young kid band from Freehold, New Jersey that I'll talk later about who had won a talent contest and the prize was they got to open for us. It was sold out that night, a thousand plus people. Norman was phenomenal as a promoter as well as a musician. You couldn't get around or over on him. He was the best piano player to come out of New Jersey. Plus, he was the smartest promoter at the time. Anyway, that kid band that won the talent contest to get to open for us that night, were called, "The Castiles." I'll talk to you later about them because they had a unique member in that band who did something huge later on that would change the music business around the world.

Anyway, I stayed with Norman and Donald I guess for a little over a year or so, doing nothing but big shows. Norman made sure, on just about everything we did that it was promoted with the biggest names in the business at the time. We worked with the Duprees, Vito and the Salutations, the Tokens, Randy and The Rainbows, You name it. Whoever was hot on the charts and radio, Norman had them in New Jersey, and we opened for them. I had met all the managers of these groups, and was picking their brains, and trying to figure out how this business works. While everybody else was just playing music for the money and girls, I was in a major learning curve to grab as much info as I could from these major acts that had made it. I knew eventually I didn't want to be on that stage performing, I wanted to be behind the scenes because that's where the money was, and that's where it was happening in my eyes and still is today. That Soul Set lasted, like I said, for a little over year and I learned a lot on what it took to get to where I wanted to be in the entertainment business, But there was still a lot more to learn but all the time I kept getting better at playing the guitar and vocally I was almost at the top of my game. But It was time for me to move on from the Soul Set. I felt I got all I could get from that experience and I had the hunger to take on the world, I just needed a little more polish. But make no mistake Norman Seldin was a major part of what I would become.

Then into my life came a guy name John Shaw and his band "The Jaywalkers" from Asbury Park, New Jersey.

A little background on John Shaw, and the Jaywalkers before we get started. At the time, the Jaywalkers were probably the top guns on the Jersey Shore as far as cover bands were concerned.

It was mainly because of John Shaw and his brilliant leadership and business savvy. Bands just didn't stay together, and still don't stay together today, but John Shaw was able through numerous personnel changes to maintain the Jaywalkers as the top club cover band on the Jersey Shore. For the record everybody that was anybody in the music field on the Jersey shore played with the Jaywalkers at one time or another. His brilliant leadership and business savvy kept that band name rolling for over 15 years straight and at the top of the pile as far as drawing power, making money and work consistency was concerned. And to my knowledge they never missed a week out of work. A feat that would have seemed impossible back then as well as today in the entertainment industry.

The way I finally got to John Shaw's band was, I had been out of work in music after I left Norman Seldin's band. So I got a part-time job at a McDonald's Hamburger place, believe it or not in Middletown, N.J. On route 35. By then I had left the hair dressing thing in Lincroft and finished the courses at Julliard and my next stop was supposed to be Berkeley College in Boston for more music training, But I put a hold on that next step and believe it or not got that job at that McDonald's.

Their hamburgers were selling for 15 cents a piece and an order of fries was 10 cents at that time. There was a guy working the grill flipping burgers named Mickey. It was his job to teach me how to work the grill because unbeknownst to Mickey they were getting ready to fire him and replace him with me. I worked with Mickey I guess for about a month before they let him go, but during that time I got to know that Mickey was a musician. At night, he was working with this band called the Jaywalkers, So, he invited me up one night to see them perform. I went up to a place called Grohs in Belmar, New Jersey and there they were, this highly touted band the Jaywalkers that I had heard so much about.

The place was packed and they were fantastic, I mean they were without a doubt the top guns and had a serious fat sound and they simply rocked the house. Mickey was great at what he did but in my personal opinion at the time, he was way over rated by the locals. He was a good singer, but you know as I watched them, I said to myself," I can do this, and I think I can probably do it better."

However I walked out that night with the greatest respect for John Shaw and his Jaywalkers, but I knew in my mind, "Hey, I'm better than Mickey is.

"Anyway, to make a long story short, some time later there was a keyboard player in the Jaywalkers named Donnie. He was a real doper. A total druggie nit wit. The guy was stoned 24-7. One night he didn't show up for a job with the Jaywalkers, and it actually was at Grohs in Belmar, (it was later revealed that Donnie was 2 blocks away in a phone booth for 3 hours and could not figure out how to get out). I got a call from John Shaw out of the blue. He said, "Listen man, ya wanna come up and sit in on the keyboard?" "Donnie didn't show up for the job." I said, "Sure.". So I went up, and sat in with them playing Keyboards, and by that time Mickey had quit the band because according to John, Mickey had found God and God told him to stop performing the devils music.

I remember talking to John, and I said," What happened to Mickey?" He said, "Oh, he found

God." Mickey was busy running around with a Bible preaching to the musicians that they were doing the devil's work by playing music on the Jersey Shore.

Anyway, in an attempt to make this story shorter, I sat in that night for Donnie, and I just knew right away this playing keyboards stuff and not singing wasn't for me. One reason was they had no bass player in the group and I had to use my left hand for the bass parts, and my left hand wasn't that strong (Let's face it at that time I was no Norman Seldin). My right hand was strong, but my left hand wasn't so I just didn't fit. So I walked away from it, and didn't see John for another 2 or 3 months.

And then I got a surprise call from John and he was shucking and jiving on the phone "Hey, Hey, Fast Eddie Ducane, I need a lead singer and you're it!!", I knew I really needed to be with John because he was doing a lot of studio work. He was constantly in the studio recording, writing new material and creating new music and styles, and that's where I needed to be if I was going to get to the top in this business.

My dream direction was not to be on stage performing, even though that was my main road into the business to move forward at this time. My real desire and goal was to be a producer behind the scenes creating that stuff. John Shaw and his Jaywalkers at that time was really in my cross hairs. I needed to get to that point of learning the ropes of recording and producing and he could get me one step closer to attaining that level.

Probably to this day, I credit the so called Sound Of Asbury Park, S.O.A.P, to John Shaw because he inadvertently without knowing it, he created that sound by changing personnel so many times in his band. Different types of musicians would come into that band, and at any given time you could have doo wop singers like Jersey Shore Legends, Niki Addeo or Leon Trent, and then there was the rock in roll players like Garry Tallent and Little Steven, and of course the stoner dope heads with the psychedelic vibe like Donnie and Eugene, and the blues guys like guitarist Billy Ryan and singers like Mickey.

Ya know there was always different players coming in and out with completely different sounds and styles. And when that all came together with the already set in place Jaywalker sound, it would somehow change the complexity of the Jaywalkers sound ever so slightly, but it was oblivious that there was magic happening in that sound, and that became the Sound of Asbury Park that really made Bruce Springsteen and Jon Bonjovi so famous.

The Sound Of Asbury Park has been credited in some circles to Springsteen and Bonjovi. Those guys didn't create it. They weren't even close. It was done 10 years before them.

So in short I joined The Jaywalkers and I replaced a singer they called Cherry Bomb, his real name was Billy Lucia. He was a great singer and for sure the ladies loved him, he kinda had that Fabian look going on with a slight touch of a "Nicky Newark" look, but again, he brought another style into the mix. Billy was like Frankie Valli from The 4 Seasons. He was that type singer, a good looking guy with a powerful voice that could hit those high power notes with ease.

Now, in comes me, who had a real black sounding soulful voice, totally different from Billy so I brought more of a soul flavor to the band. I went up and sang with them one night, and me and John just hit it off. I mean, we were tight. He used to give everybody nicknames. And right from the start he hit me with, "Hey hey hey fast Eddie Ducane, you're in!" And I got in the band, and while I was with the band we went through probably 7 or 8 personnel changes.

When I started in the band the keyboard player was Jay Pilling. Jay played the electric organ, he was good at it, he got the job done. He did just what was needed no more no less, But he filled in those gaps perfectly, another member was a guitar player called Gary Arntz, mediocre at best, definitely no Billy Ryan who was the hot gun on guitar at the time. John Shaw on the drums, with me singing lead, I had dropped the guitar at that point and was just singing. It was more or less a power trio type thing, Jay did the left handed bass on the keys. John, was on the drums, BUT mind you he'll never go down in the Hall of Fame as a drummer. He stood up and played, He never sat down. He did alright, He kept the beat solid but He wasn't a hard driving flash drummer. There wasn't a whole lot going on, back on the drums. BUT he sang his ass off, he was great in that department, and he was very British orientated so back then that sound went a long way. In a way, I think he pictured himself being a John Lennon in more ways than just music.

Anyway, that group stayed together for a while, and then there was another personnel change. John added Garry Tallent as a bass player/ guitar player combination. He also added a local guy called Miami Steve Van Zandt . Steve was playing the electric piano back then and those two players once again brought in another different musical style to the Jaywalkers overall sound. The funny thing about those two guys was, they would later go on to be in Bruce Springsteens legendary East Street Band. Which just goes to prove that many of the players that came through the Jaywalkers went on to some large degree of greatness.

We (The Jaywalkers) were playing at a place called, Steve Brodie's. It was just across the street from the boardwalk and ocean, on the strip in Asbury Park. It was the dead of winter, and we were still drawing people like crazy. I mean it was just packed all the time. In one of the instances that I remember from that time was when man first landed on the moon and it was televised around the world. We took a break, and everybody was watching the television in the bar area of the club and the guy was just getting ready to walk on the moon. The first step on the moon. The astronaut was climbing down the ladder from the space capsule and just before he took his first step on the moon, George who was the manger there, came up to John and says, "Come on play man!" "There's people in here!" And John said, "They're getting ready to step on the moon!" He said, "I don't give a shit!" "Get up there and play!" I don't think John ever forgot that? For years later he said, "You remember we couldn't see the first step on the moon because we had to play for that ass hole George." That was just one of the events that took place at Steve Brodie's but I will say the nights we performed at Steve Brodies, that's a whole other book.

There was also a guy that came in there all the time. His name was Tom Potter. Tom was a hair dresser like I used to be. So me and Tom got together a lot and talked when he came in. But when he came in, he always came in with a girl he was dating by the name of Margaret. She was like a hippie looking girl, ya know, With the slouch bent up leather hat and all that beads and flower stuff going on and she had aspirations of becoming a singer ( I Think she thought she was the next Janis Joplin). Only problem was she was terrible as a singer, and Tom would bring her around to all these clubs, and have her sit in with the hopes that one of the bands would take her in as a singer.

Well, Tom would come in Steve Brodie's probably 3 times a week with her, and she would sing the same God damn song every time, "Mustang Sally." After a while, John Shaw would see him come in the door, and would look at me and say "Oh no, here we go! Margaret Mustang Freakin' Sally. And she'd get up there and sing as best she could.

Well, one night, she was up there singing her song, "Mustang Freakin' Sally", and I was talking to Tom and he says, "Eddie, what do ya think about me opening up a coffee house?" Back then, coffee houses were not really big anymore, they were big back in the Beatnik era in the Village in New York City during the late 50's and the very early 60's, but that had since died out. Those coffee houses in the city were the place to go hear poetry, folk singers, progressive music and anything that was outside the box of what was so called normal at the time. Tom's idea was to open up a coffee house in Asbury

Park and this way it would attract musicians to jam, and he could possibly get a band together for Margaret to sing with and play at this coffee house. She wound up never playing at any of the clubs around Asbury that he had brought her to and I might add never got any of the bands to take her on as a singer, but that's what he wanted to do so that's what he did.

He build this coffee house, and called it, "The Upstage Club." because It was on top of a two story building. And old Tom sure enough did put that band together behind her and they sure as hell played at The Upstage Club. Only a funny thing happened after 1:00 am or 2 am all the musicians playing the clubs on the shore didn't have anyplace to go, they would wind up at The Upstage and jam, oh yea and add the fact that Tom would give them free beer (He only served soft drinks at the Upstage, but always had a case or 3 of beer in the back). Later on it became known as the place that inspired all these musicians that became famous from the Jersey Shore. That's a bunch of bullshit! But There was no place else to go if you were not getting laid by some groupie you wound up at the Upstage.

And another funny thing happened, there was one particular guitar player that went up there a lot and was introduced to the club by one of the hot drummers at the time Vini "MadDog" Lopez, Vinnie had a group at one time called The

Moment Of Truth. The reason this young guitar player went up there to begin with was, Vini had seen him playing at an Italian American club in Long Branch and Vini was impressed and invited him up there to jam and because he was too young to go in the bars, but he could go to the Upstage and play. His name was Bruce Springsteen. He'd go up there and jam. Ya know, for free, he just loved to play that kid. Tom never paid him or anybody anything other than free beer.

I myself wasn't particularly into jamming or free beer and to this day I'm still not in to it, so I went there maybe once or twice, and that was it. Like I told you, my goal was to be a producer. Period. I was with the Jaywalkers for one reason only, and that reason was for John Shaw to get me into recording studios.

So anyway, The Upstage Club was going on, There was another coffee house that opened in Long Branch called the Ink Well, and everything music wlse was happening on the Jersey shore, It was on fire during that time. 12 months a year 7 night a week, non stop. But I was happy working with John and finally John decided out of a clear blue sky, "Okay, Fast Eddie we're gonna go into a studio."

We went to Philadelphia, Pa. to a place called, Virtue Recording Studio, that was owned by a guy called, Frank Virtue. Frank Virtue was a part of a group called “The Virtues” that had a number one record back in the day called, “Guitar Boogie Shuffle.”

We got to the studio that night and we were ready to start cutting some new material, but before we started, there were 2 other artists/acts scheduled to come in before us. One was Eddie Holman. He recorded a song called, “Hey There Lonely Girl.” There was a part in the song where he tried to hit a high note at the very end of the song, and he couldn’t hit the note, it was out of his range. This would be my first time I got to witness studio tricks or studio magic as it was known and I later became a master at it.

One thing that was different back then vs today was they were recording on tape vs today that’s done on a computer hard disc. I watched them as they physically put their hand on the reel of the tape as it was going around to slow it down so he could hit this note which was lower in pitch because when the tape slowed down the pitch of the song became lower. When they slowed it down, it dropped the key of the song, and he sang it in that key and hit a note Then they played it back, and then picked their hand up which caused the tape to run faster at it’s normal speed and the note he sang now was a lot higher. So it was almost like a Chipmunk sounding note, but not that electronic sounding. So they tried to do that I guess 15 or 16 times, and they finally got it right. The ironic thing in that studio which was unlike today, there was no headsets, or headphones. So in another words, you listened to the music track coming through to you on a little small speaker in front of you on the wall, and with no headsets, it was all sorta live!!. Or, you could also record live with the band straight to an acetate record which was an actual record made of metal and covered with a layer of vinyl and it cut the grooves as you were recording, so it was a one take deal no do overs, no retakes when recording to acetate.

Talking about Eddie Holman's "Hey There Lonely Girl." If you listen to the song at the end when he hits an unbelievable high note. That's not really him. That' s not Eddie hitting it, oh he's singing it alright but he sang it 2 keys lower. The funny part about it is he did a radio interview about 3 weeks later with a DJ called, Jerry Blavat and in the interview Jerry said, "Let me hear ya hit that note at the end of the song!" I remember listening to the interview saying," Oh shit!" "That ain't gonna fly!" Anyway, Eddie talked his way out of doing it.

The next group after Eddie was a group called the Stylistics. The Stylistics were a black singing group from Philly, and they came in and did a song called, "You're a Big Girl Now, No More Daddy's Little Girl." At the time when you wanted to use orchestration, violins and things like that on your recording in Philadelphia, everyone used The Philadelphia Phil Harmonic Orchestra which gave those recordings that different sound known as TSOP, (The Sound Of Philadelphia).

Anyway, this group came in, the Stylistics, and they started to record and it was time to bring the strings in. Well, it turned out that they didn't have enough money to pay the violin players so Frank said, "Well, we're just gonna go with it the way it is with a rhythm section" so they were forced to sing it live, One Take with the band. The ironic part of that song was, it was released on Atco Embassy Records and it started them on a career that included 10 or so number one hit records. Go Figure, that first record they did with only 3 instruments on it because they couldn't afford anymore instruments on it, lead them into legendary status in the entertainment business.

So that was my first studio experience with John Shaw, and it was pretty cool because I got to see some of the tricks and things that went on behind the scenes that the buying public never knew about. The learning experience was phenomenal for me.

We went back to Asbury Park, and The

Jaywalkers would sometimes have maybe 2 days off some weeks. We'd work Tuesday through Saturday which would give us Sunday and Monday off. That gave us a chance to go see other musicians. Me and John would hang out, and go see other bands. We went to one place I can remember called The Howell Lanes. This guy Jack Valentine, who was an ex- Jaywalker guitar player had his band playing there. I listened to him, and I remember John saying. "Hey Hey Fast Eddie What do ya think of Valentine?" I said, "I think he's fantastic!" He said, "What!" are you crazy "He ain't no hot guitar player!" I said, "The hell he ain't!" What he's doing is, he's mastered the down stroke". Most guitar players when they strike the guitar string they'll strike down and up, down and up in a strumming motion. Jack only struck it down, but he had mastered that so well using his left to either hold the chord tight against the neck to make it sustain or release it and muffle it that helped him get a more punchy rhythmic pattern which replaced the holes in the song so it didn't get empty spots and lose that punch. That impressed me with Jack, he kept that sound full and moving.

The next week we went to a place that was right down the street from where we were playing. We went actually on a break. We were playing at a hot club called, "The Pillow Talk" that was owned by this really cool guy named Chico. Maybe sixty steps away was a small little club. Our club where we were playing was a huge club, but this other club that I mentioned was a little shit hole in the wall club called, "The Student Prince". We walked down to the Student Prince, and we couldn't get in. They were mobbed with a line outside the door, and it was all college kids from Monmouth University in Long Branch. So me and John stood at the door looking in and I remember the band (The Moment Of Truth) were doing this song, I think it was a remake of the song, "Keep Me Hangin On the Supremes song, BUT they were doing it in a hard rock style. I mean these guys were kickin' ass and rockin' hard. They were tearing holes in the place, and these kids were eatin' it up. I remember saying, "John, That's the future of rock in roll on the Jersey Shore!" Which, later went on to be a big term describing a guy that would play that club a year later with a band called "Child", Bruce Springsteen.

Remember I told you about that group that opened for us at the Matawan Roller Rink when I was with Norman Seldin on that Rascal show that was called the Castiles who had won the talent contest to open for us, and I told you there was a key member in there. Well that key member was now at the Student Prince, and his name was and still is Bruce Springsteen.

When Bruce's band played in there a lot of things were about to change on the Jersey Shore when it came to the material (songs) that bands played and the cover bands were playing in the clubs.

So, moving on from there, everything kept moving along as planned, and John's next step was to take me to New York City. A studio called The Record Plant because he wanted to get a specific vocal sound that was recorded by a group called Vanilla Fudge, and they recorded at the Record Plant.

Record Plant was a major major recording studio. We showed up at the Plant, and now I' m really with the heavy weights in the industry in the studio. We're in studio A, and studio B was a group called Mountain with Felix Pappalardi and Leslie West. Upstairs is a group that I opened for years ago, The Rascals." And, when we're leaving, in comes this guy named Jimi Hendrix. So we're really in the thick of it at the Record Plant. And that in my mind probably culminated my deal with John Shaw cause after that point, I had taken that relationship with The Jaywalkers as far as I could take it and as far as they could take me, and it was time for me to go out on my own. But, before I went out on my own, I had to make sure I had all my bases covered and all my ducks in a row. Once I knew I had gotten all I could from that scenario it was time to move on.

# Mafia, Mobsters, and Music
## (And a Splash of Canada)

My time with the Jaywalkers had reached its end. I felt that I had gotten everything I could get out of that situation. It was great while it lasted, but again, I had to remind myself that I had reached my goals and dreams and needed to continue to move forward. I think the Jaywalkers had settled into a rut of being you know "The number one bar band of the Jersey Shore."'

I wanted to be the producer of the world, not just the Jersey Shore. It was time for me to re-access my direction, and figure out how I could get to the next level. It was obvious at that point, to me, that I knew at this time in my life that I had reached the top of the entertainment game as a stage performer, singer, guitar player and an entertainer as far as I was concerned. It might have been the right time for me to start my own thing instead of being just a band member.

So, I did just that. I formed my own touring band, and wanted to get out of the Jersey Shore and start to take shows in different states. But before that happened, I had to play in known territory where I had established a following. To be honest with you, I felt I already had a huge established following on the Jersey Shore.

One thing about the Jersey Shore is that not many people realized or knew that organized crime was at the top of the food chain in both Jersey entertainment and business. Organized crime figures and families owned most of the clubs, and without a doubt they owned every damn jukebox in almost every state. Jukebox's were the third biggest exposure venue an artist could achieve other than radio and television.

Names likeVito "Don Vito" Genovese, Pussy Russo, Charley the Blade, Dutchie Torene to name just a few were always popping up behind closed doors in the entertainment industry. The marriage between organized crime and musicians was very strong. Remember I told you about in the last chapter where Bruce Springsteen was playing Italian American clubs? Well, there was a huge element in those clubs that were mobster related. So, the relationship between musicians and mobsters was pretty tight. A lot of mobsters also had entertainment management companies as well as record labels for the mob connected entertainers. Music more or less became a front for organized crime.

It was during that time, that we were also introduced to horse racing. You say, "What the hell does horse racing got to do with music?" Well, there was a jockey the time, and his name was, Barry Pearl. He was the leading "bug boy" in the country. When I say "bug boy" that means he was a rookie in his first year race riding, and was allowed to ride with less weight in the saddle, which in short, gave him an advantage. The less weight you carried the faster your horse went, or so the expert handicappers say.

It was Barry's first year racing, and he was winning races like crazy. He also had a great hidden desire to be a singer. I was playing a club called, "Port a Call" in Long Branch that was owned by two ex- cops from Long Branch, New Jersey. Barry would come in, and sing a few songs with us. I got pretty tight with him. So did the mobsters. That's when I found out horse racing wasn't 100 percent legit. They used to make a joke about it. I would say, "Is this shit for real?" Their answer would always be, "It's more honest than baseball!" Mocking that baseball was also fixed. Anyway, Barry would come in and sing, and sooner or later I got involved in that end of what was called "The Sport Of Kings". Jockeys could not bet on horses themselves legally. It was against the law, so Barry asked me to do him a favor one night, and go the race track and bet on some of the horses for him. There would be a signal Barry would give me when he came out of the paddock just before he entered the main race track, if he wanted me to bet his money on the horse he was riding.They would parade the horses in the paddock, and come out on the track. When he saw me on the side, his signal would be to stand up on the saddle and tighten his saddle strap. That was the signal to bet on him in that race. Needless to say, we all made tons of money. That's right, I said TONS OF MONEY, at those racetracks! No matter where he went to race, we were there! And before you know it, other jockeys were coming into the circle, and other mobsters were also cashing in. BUT, me and my boys were there in the fix.

There was a certain way you had to bet too. Ya didn't go right up and bet $3000.00 to win because it would change the odds too quick, and the odds would drop at the track fast. The people that were at the track would see those odds plummet, and they'd get on it knowing that a big bet was placed and a big bet like that would take a long shot and bring it down to a favorite, so driving the odds down would decrease the big payoff. Sometimes if the odds were short. We would "lay off" the bet to a bookie so the odds did not reflect the big bet at the track.

So that was, believe it or not, another side of the music business or should I say, "Another perk that came from it.

In the meantime, we were rolling in money, fast woman, and all the fake shit that money brings. On the plus side, we were traveling so much to different race tracks, I was also starting to branch out into other states as an entertainer. I would try to do some shows wherever we were at the time. At that time, a lot of the hotels. Holiday Inn, Ramada, and Sheraton all had bands performing in them. I would go to those towns and states to make horse bets, and wind up sitting in and performing there. My reputation on the road as an entertainer started to build, because I was kickin ass in every club.

During this time, I always maintained my desire to also continue to produce records. The money I had gotten from the races enabled me to get into the studios more and more, and perfect my craft.

Around that time I was referred by a friend, to a guy called, Cedric. He lived in Rumson, New Jersey. Rumson, New Jersey, for those of you who don't know, was an extremely high class area. An expensive area to live in with house's back then running into the millions of dollars. Cedric, I was told, had a guy he wanted me to record, and that would also give me a chance to produce a record on a new artist. So I went up and met with him, and it was then that I discovered that Cedric was a very old man. He had something to do with the Newark Star Ledger newspaper. It was the largest newspaper in New Jersey. He was an extremely very wealthy old man for sure, but he was also very gay at the time. This guy that he wanted me to produce was one of his girl friends (boyfriend) boy toy. Back then, gay isn't like it is today where it's understood and accepted in most circles. Back then it was very underground. The name the guy that was going to record was Twiggy. He had another young guy friend name Bobby Bear that they called, "Teddy Bear." So here we have two gay guys that are young and very flamboyant, and good looking I might add. They're like 21 or 22 years of age, and Cedric, who was like a decrepit old dirty man, was like 80 years old. Anyway, he wanted to put the money up for Twiggy to record a record. So I produced a song in a studio for Twiggy in the Soho district of the village in New York . That song was originally recorded by Johnny Rivers. It was called,"Summer Rain." So we take Twiggy and his crew in the studio in New York, and produce a record on him. It was difficult working with him! I mean the guy could not carry a tune to save his life! They were just completely, for lack of a better word, drag queens without getting dressed. Okay? They could not sing s damn note! But here's when the first studio tricks came into use. With hours of work on his vocals, we got the record done and it sounded damn good. He could never duplicate it live, because it was all studio tricks making him sound good. I charged Cedrick $2,000.00 to do the record.

Five or six weeks had gone by, and they were playing this damn record in all the big gay clubs in New York. This guy Twiggy was getting a buzz going with the gay community in Manhattan, New York, and I hadn't gotten paid for it yet. So I went to Cedric's house one night, and I just said, "Ah Cedrick, I need to get paid my money!" Ya have to remember now, I'm hanging around with all these mobsters so now my personality has changed to a tough guy. That particular night I had a gun with me as I always carried one at the time. And by the way, I still do today. Old habits die hard. It was in a shoulder harness/ holster under my coat. I said, "Cedrick, ya know I need my money." "Ya know, it's been 5 or 6 weeks." He had Bobby Bear and Twiggy there, and he laughed and said, "Well why don't we just take it out trade?" And I went off on em. I pulled the gun out, and stuck the gun right in his mouth, and he started to choke from the gun being in his mouth. I said," You've got 24 hours mother fucker, or I'm gonna open you up like a ripe fuckin' watermelon!" And I left. Whether I would have shot him or not, that's still up in the air. It's a big question mark. The jury is still out on that answer, but I did threaten him pretty hard. In the meantime, that night, Twiggy and Teddy Bear went back to Manhattan, New York. Cedric was alone in his house. He got robbed in a home invasion because he had tremendous amounts of high priced antiques in the house. Five days before that, one of the wise guys, Frankie, had asked me in Long Branch, "Has he got a lot of antiques in that house?" I replied, "Yes," but didn't think any further on the subject. Well that night, he gets robbed. I had a good idea who did the robbery, but in the meantime, the stupid ass's shot the son of a bitch and killed him. The next thing ya know, I get a warrant for my arrest for questioning in Cedric's murder. Seems that Twiggy and Teddy Bear had told the cops I had threaten him that afternoon. Now there is no way I can go and tell the cops anything. I can't even go and talk to them about what I knew about the robbery, or who was involved. I had no other choice, but to leave the state of New Jersey quickly. Real damn quick! And that's what I did. I went non-stop to Florida to hide out. My world now was totally upside down.

When I was in Florida, I quickly put a band together. We started to tour, and I mean we toured a lot. You name the club, if they had music in it, we played it. And now instead of Eddie DuCane, it had now morphed into the name Doc Holiday. BUT, I stayed as clear of New Jersey as possible.

The name Doc Holiday had a double edge to it. Back then, the agents that we're booking us called us the Doc Holiday Band. People, not like today, knew who Doc Holiday was with the Wyatt Earp story. Back then they didn't connect it, but the name was familiar to them. They knew they had heard the name. They didn't associate it with a Kevin Costner movie as we do today. So, when the agency would call a club owner up, and said, "Listen, do you have this week open?" They replied," Yeah, we're open this week." "Who ya got?" "We have Doc Holiday." And the club owner would go, "Oh, yeah yeah, I've heard of him!" They didn't hear of me because I had just gotten to Florida, and just started using that name. It was just because that name was familiar to them that we got into the clubs. And when we got in, we tore them up!

I had a back up band out of Huntsville, Alabama called, Thunder Chicken. People used to say to me, "How did they get that name, Thunder Chicken?" Well, I was looking for a band while I was in Florida, and an agent name Hugh Rogers based out of Atlanta, Georgia told me, "Listen, there's this band in Huntsville, Alabama if you wanna go hear them?" "They may be what your looking for?" And I did. We drove from Miami to

Atlanta and then to Huntsville, Alabama to listen to them play on this farm where they were practicing in a huge deserted chicken coup in the middle of nowhere. So we're riding down a dirt road in the middle of this corn field, and I remember one of the agents in the car said, "Man it sounds like thunder comin' out of that God damn chicken coup." It was a huge chicken coup! It sounded like thunder coming out of there because they had huge Voice of the Theater speakers, and the band was as powerful as I had ever heard.They were just a bunch of good old country boys that could rock their ass's off! So that's where the name, "Thunder Chicken" came from. So we put that band together, and we're playing all along southern Alabama, the Florida panhandle, throughout Louisiana and Mississippi, and jumped back and forth into Georgia. We're doing great! I mean we're killing em' in every club! We're knock em' dead! This was one hot ass band that inspired me every damn night. Then all of a sudden I became a great lead singer because of the inspiration I got from the band. They pushed me every night, and they pushed hard. We do a show in Pensacola, Florida at a place called The Beachcomber. While I'm in Pensacola, I called my agent Hugh Rogers. I said, "Listen, a guy is here at the show, and they want to hire us to play in Nova Scotia, Canada." I was all for it. Ya know, cause that's stretching me out into a wider area of exposure. So he said, "Ya can't do that man" "Ya can't go up there!" "They got Eskimos up there!" "If something happens, we can't protect ya!" And I said, "Well listen, they're paying us $4,800.00 a week!" "Ya know, I'm going!" He said, "Well you're on your own!" So, we closed in Pensacola on a Sunday night, and we drove from Pensacola, Florida to the Maine/Canadian border crossing going into Canada. It took us 2 damn days, but in the meantime, when I'm going up there, instead of going the normal route which would be interstate 95 through New Jersey, I went around New Jersey because I was afraid I was gonna get stopped, and they were gonna say, "Listen, you're wanted for questioning for this murder." So we went around New Jersey through Pennsylvania and into Canada which took us a lot longer to get there. When we finally get into Canada, and I swear we drove for 2 days hard to get up there cause we're towing another car and U Haul trailers. Those black beauties (speed) were flying! WIthout them pocket rockets, we would have never made it. The drugs were at the top of their game now. I needed them, I wanted them, I loved them! Anyway, the place we were booked at was called, "The Misty Moon." It was located on 16 and a half Gottingham Street in Halifax, Nova Scotia. We finally got there at 2:00 in the afternoon, and I might add, we are all beat to hell from driving 2 days without a break. So we're driving down Gottingham Street looking out the van window, and there's #13, 14, 15, 15 1/2, 16, and there's an empty lot! There's nothing there! I said, "Oh shit!" "I got the whole band, 3 vans, and all this equipment, and we could be fucked at this point!" So I call Hugh Rogers up in Atlanta, Georgia. I said, "Hugh, there's no fuckin club up here!" "It's an empty lot!" He said, "I told ya!" "I told ya don't go the fuck up there!" I said, "Well, we're here now!" "What do we do now?" He said, "What's the club owner's name?" So I gave him the club owner's name off the contract and his phone number. The club owner was named, Terry. Hugh said, "All right, get a motel room." "Put everybody up in a motel, and I'll get back to you." So, just for the record, there was no motels in Halifax. We had to cross the river to a town called, Dartmouth. There was a Holiday Inn there, and I put all my guys in there. We're traveling with 12 people. I put everybody up in the hotel, and of course sooner or later we're gonna run out of money. Ya know, it's starting to get crazy now. Finally, Hugh calls me back up and he says, "All right, just sit tight man, and we'll work all this out." I said, "O K.", but by this time I'm really in a panic mode, We're sitting there for 4 days, and the hotel bills and food bills are running up. I said to myself, "Oh man, we're not even gonna get out of this country!" Ya know, we're running out of money, and Hugh says,

"Relax Man." "I Got this." The next night, a Friday Night, there was a knock on my door. Here's this little Greek guy, and he said, "Doc Holiday?" I said, "Yeah." He said, "My name is Terry." "I own the Misty Moon." I said, "Oh man." "What's happening?" "What's going on?" He hands me an envelope, and there's $4800.00 in cash in the envelope. He said, "We'll be opened next week." I said, "Opened next week?" "There's not even a club there?" He said, "We're building it now, and we'll be ready to go by Wednesday." I said, "Ok." So I take the $4800.00, and pay the hotel rooms, the food bills and the guys salary for the week. Now we're OK.Terry gave me his phone number, and I call him up a few days later and said, "All right Terry, it's Tuesday, when can we load in?" He said, "No, No, it won't be till Friday." In the meantime, I get in the car, and me and two of my roadies Blake and Travis drive over. Sure enough it wasn't a vacant lot anymore. They actually got a club built there. A two story club at that! It's huge, but the inside is not finished. So I go back to Dartmouth. I said, "Guys, I think we're gonna play this thing." "They have like 50 workers on this bitch trying to get it opened.

Well sure enough Friday afternoon they opened that bitch up. We went in there with Thunder Chicken. These good old Southern boys from Alabama. I'm telling you, we tore the place apart. We were the hottest thing since slice bread in Canada! And before we could get out the club, we were booked for 11 weeks straight, and $4800.00 a week all across the maritimes Canada. I said," I'm not even going back to the United States with this kinda money!" At that time the Canadian dollar was worth more than the American dollar. Ok, we're talking during the Nixon Administration. People in the USA didn't realize that our dollar was worth less than the Canadian dollar. Our economy was shot to shit. So I said," Pay us in Canadian funds." So here we go... We start touring Canada ,and the next thing ya know, we're in every newspaper possible, and every magazine possible. We are all over the place. OK, well before ya know it, we were crisscrossing Canada from Vancouver to Newfoundland. Now Newfoundland, that was another shot in our American asses. When we first went there, I remember the agent Skip York telling us there's 10 women for every guy. And that was correct. Ah, the reason for that is that there was no work in Newfoundland. It was very poor. The guys that lived there left the island to get jobs which left a whole lot of horny women around. However, the bad part was that out of every 10 girls or 8 girls to every guy, 6 of them were really rough. Maybe there would be 1 or 2 that were rated a 7 or 8, but that's just my opinion. So anyway we were playing across Canada back and forth and really doing good. Because probably we were the only hot American band in the country at the time. Well when the word got out that the American dollar was deflating under Nixon and losing it's value, before ya know it, there was tons of American bands in Canada. And they were high powered bands. Bands like Machine Company of Chicago which was a 10 piece funk horn band that kicked ass, a six piece girl band from China called, "The China Dolls." They had a pretty unique show cause they opened up their show playing bag pipes playing Amazing Grace. I know it sounds corny right now, but it was pretty awesome when they did it. Before ya know it, there were American groups all over the place. And again, they were all high powered groups, well most of them were anyway. So, we had our competition set up for us, but ya know, we were just guys playing Southern rock and roll just tearing it up coast to coast.

There was a lot of American bands that weren't so hot. I remember one guy I came across. I'm still friends with him today (at least I was until this book came out). I love him to death, however. I'm speaking to you talent wise. His name was, and still is Johnny Green. Johnny Green and the Green Men. They were a band that wasn't that talented. Musically they weren't nothing to write home about. However, Johnny Green was a brilliant business man. He was like a used car salesman. I mean he could talk, and he relied on gimmicks to get himself over on stage. One of the gimmicks was they all had green hair, which in those days, was unheard of. They ALL had green hair! Every member of the band. But in lack of the talent, he would have magicians in his group. One guy was Doug Henning. He became a very famous magician. John himself would be eating fire on stage. So the music, ya know, wasn't there. But, the gimmicks were there. As we all know, gimmicks don't last. OK? Beanie babies and Hula hoops are a thing of the past. Ya know the talent will always survive. John got a part in, (it wasn't even apart actually). Anyway, he got the whole band in as extras on the Batman television show. And ya know as extras ya get paid $45.00 and a box lunch. Well he and his band at the time were on the screen for about 4 minutes in only one episode, and he managed to take that 4 minutes, and build it into a whole career as if he was a main actor on that show. And on that episode called, "Surf's Up," if you ever see it on a DVD, you'll see the green haired guys are standing behind the main actors. They don't actually speak any lines at all. They don't actually play anything. They don't actually do anything. They just stand there, and make faces. They're just extras. They were supposed to be the Joker's gang with green hair. He managed to take that 4 minutes, and build a career as "Batman's Own Johnny Green." But, John also had a problem of stretching the truth. BUT, he did it in places where nobody could verify him. So he would go to places like Newfoundland. It was way out of the way of mainstream, and he would tell people that he wrote the Batman theme, and blah, blah blah in three minutes. And he was friends with, oh yeah, he was the spokesperson for Bob Hope. Ya know, I mean, he had a partner called, Marty Conn. He was the biggest bullshit artist in the history of the entertainment business. Everybody knew him as a total asshole. John teamed up with this moron. So, that's how John got over, and still gets over today. So anyway, John finds these out-of- the-way places in the world, and goes in as Batman's own Johnny Green. Ya know, 4 minutes as an extra on a television show, and ya build a whole career out of it. But like I said,"I love the guy." The best part, he's still doing it today. The same way. That is, until they figure him out. So God bless him... If there is a God? The jury is still out on that for me anyway.

So back to us. We're in Canada, and we're really performing a lot. We're making a ton of money, but we're working maybe a little too much. The band was getting a little stale, and the drugs and booze were starting to take its toll. We were now touring Canada for a couple of years without a break, and I thought it was time to move on because the bottom line was I still wanted to produce records and not be a performer. Ya know, that was my whole thing from the start. Dreams go on forever, we just run out of time, and I was not going to run out of time. I didn't want to be an entertainer. Although I was good at it, I used that as a vehicle to step up to what I wanted to do. So anyway, we all decided we were gonna leave Canada. The band Thunder Chicken went back to Alabama, and I went back to Miami, Florida. We all left on great terms and we all thought that part of our lives were over, and it would never happened again. I wound up hanging out in Fort Lauderdale getting stoned every damn day, and going through money like it was water. I guess about 8 weeks? I went crazy. I had to get back on the road. So, I called the agent, Skip York, in Halifax, Nova Scotia. I said, "Skip, book us out." "I'm coming back." And he did. He booked us out for like 22 weeks. I called the band in Alabama, and I said," You guys wanna run again?" There was a moment of silence on the phone, and they said,"Yeah." I said, "OK, meet me at the ferry boat in Sydney, Nova Scotia to take the boat over to Newfoundland." "We got a 22 week tour." I drove up there by myself non stop from Miami talking on the CB radio, pumpin' in coffee, and eating pocket rockets. That was the days of "black beauties." "speed". I mean, I made it in 2 days! Never closed my eyes once. That speed/ meth was running through my blood, Shit I was ready to take on the world... or so I thought. I didn't know if the band was gonna be there or not? And really, after two days of doing meth, I really didn't care. I mean, after all, I just talked to them during that one phone call. But they did say, "Yeah." I got to Sydney, Nova Scotia, and the boat was there. I was wired, but sure enough, there was the truck from Alabama. The boys were there. We got on the boat, and headed out to Newfoundland. We did another tour, and this time we really tore that island up! I guess the little time off mixed with the drugs made us push the music stronger than ever? It was unbelievably better than the first time we were in, and that time we were really strong. So, we came back like rock stars up there. I started doing a lot of television interviews up there, and I did the Elwood Glover Show which was probably similar to the Phil Donahue show here. Of course my attitude and mouth flew off the handle, and I said shit that constantly got us in trouble...once again, thanks to the drugs and booze. Like the one time I was asked on TV, "Well what do ya think of the female Canadian singers up here?" I said, "Well in the United States they would be nothing but converted go go girls" "They all sucked!" That didn't go over very well. I mean we had death threats for Christ sake! We were doing a lot of newspaper interviews, and I would always say something that would offend somebody out there. Ya know? But hey, that was me... or was it the drugs talking? That was my personality. Plus the fact I was stoned 24/7. That's what they liked about me, I guess? Or at leaset some of them did. And because of the drugs, I shot from the hip without thinking anything through.

At the end of the 22 weeks, it was over. It was time to move on. What I did was, we got to the border, and we made a lot of money. I mean really! We made a ton of money. I crossed the border with 80 grand in cash in a suitcase. But there was a lot of crazy stuff that went on during that time including meeting a girl at a performance in New Glasgow, Nova Scotia at the Peter Pan Club. She was in the club during the sound check in the afternoon by herself listening, and I walked up to her, and laid the worst line in the world on her. I said, "What"s a nice girl like you doing in a place like this?" I started talking to her, and asked if she was coming to the show that night? She said no, she was getting married. That's right, you heard me. Getting married! So anyway, I said," I'm Doc Holiday." She said, "I know who you are." "I seen your picture in the paper." She was a hot little number, and as a joke I said, "We're pullin' out after the show at 2:00 am if ya wanna forget about that married shit be here, and go to Miami with me." She laugh, and I walked away. We did the show that night, and we were sold out! After the show, I went to my room to pack so we could hit the road. One of my roadies came in and said, "Hey Boss, you know that broad you was talking to this afternoon?" I said, "Yeah, that little blond broad?" He said, "Yeah well she's out by the bus waitin' on you!" I said, "Bring her back here." He did, and me and her hooked up right away. The next thing I knew, she was on the bus heading out with me. It was that quick. That was 40 years ago, and she's still here. I remember when she left Canada with me. People in that town were saying, "She'll come back in a box." Her brother, Vernon, was the worst of all of them, He had nothing to say good about her leaving with me. But I guess that was their way of making a good thing seem bad. Well, it's been close to 40 years now, she's still here, my best friend and for the people in that town still waiting for her to come back in a box, she owns a one million dollar house in Virginia, drives an $80,000.00 new Corvette, and has done quite well as my wife and more so as my best friend!

Well we got to the border, and I went back to Miami. I was in Miami for a couple of months, and me and the band actually never spoke or seen each other again to this day. I really don't know why cause we were all like brothers. It just would never happen again. That page in all our lives was over for some reason. Eventually, I said, "I gotta get back out!" I threw together a little four piece band, but because of my drug problem I was difficult to work with so I change players a lot. Some great players came through the ranks at that time. Guys like Ray Harris, Myron Hale,

Kenny Parker Paul "Gerber" Pizon, Snookie Earl, Eric Ness, and Frank Rosa. I mean really great players. I started playing in the states. Virginia, South Carolina, Georgia, Alabama, Mississippi, and Texas. I was all over the place. But, ya know, I was doing really well with it, but the drugs were still in the picture now more than ever. Then I got booked in a place called, "The Domino Lounge" in Dedham, Massachusetts. Little did I know that this would be a huge turning point in my career. The Domino Lounge was a little neighborhood bar. I remember when we got there a day early, I walked in and they had a DJ performing. His name was Jimmy Jay. I'll never forget it. I walked into the club, and it was packed! I mean this guy was packing the club! He had a suit on that was covered in albums. Vinyl albums. Ya couldn't see his body. He looked like a walking vinyl album. Probably 100 vinyl album stuck to this suit he had on. I'm saying, "What the hell is this?" And then, he had a Go Go girl who had a body suit on, and she had 45 records tacked to her body. You couldn't see her body. She looked like a female walking 45 vinyl record. I watched them for about 2 hours, and I said, "This guy is phenomenal!" I mean he's unbelievable! And then the middle of the night, he introduces an act of his who was an Elvis impersonator. The guy was about 50 years old. He's bald, he's got an Elvis jumpsuit on, and probably weighs about 390 pounds. And I'm saying, "I can't believe that this shit is going on!" The people were loving it! Well anyway, we got booked in the Domino Lounge for a week. I went in there to worked there for a week, and wound up working there for 6 weeks.

While I was there Jimmy said, "Listen man, I want you to come down and play this club in South Boston called The Triple O's. So I went down to South Boston with him, and looked at this club. It was a little small club, and the guy's name that owned it was Kevin O Neal. He said, "I want ya to play my club." Almost like an order. I said, "Ok." They really didn't have bands in that club. They had DJ's. Ya know, Jimmy played in it all the time. We went in, and we played it 6 nights a week. We tore the place apart. I mean it was just great. These people were coming in, and I just said to Jimmy one night, "Jimmy, listen." "I don't wanna do this shit anymore." "I wanna make records!" He said, "I'm gonna take you over to meet a guy that has some money." I said," Ok." So he comes over, he picks me up, and we go to Somerville, Massachusetts. It's a body and fender place, and a beat up one at that. I said, "Wait a minute!" "Ya bringing me to a fucking body shop?" He said, "Yeah, I want you to meet this guy." So anyway, I walk in, and a guy meets us at the door. Jimmy says to him, "This is Doc Holiday." And the guy at the door said,"I know who he is, man." "I like your music man." And I said," And you're?" And he goes," Steve Flemmi." "They call me "The Rifleman." I said, "Ok". So now I'm in dejavu of the New Jersey mobster days. They walk me back into this small office, and there's a small guy with slicked back hair sitting behind a desk. I walk in, and he says, "You're Doc Holiday." I said, "Yep." He said, "I understand you wanna get into a recording studio and make records." I said, "Yeah, I'm looking for a backer that will help me out." He stands up and says, "I'm that guy." And I said, "Ok, cool." He said, "My name is Whitey Bolger." And then he said, "And from now on, I manage you." I said, "Well I really don't need a..." And I didn't get the sentence out. He said, "Did you hear what I said?" "From now on, I fuckin' mange you!" "And from now on, you're connected in this state." "And you don't get a parking ticket." "You don't get a speeding ticket." "You don't get any heat what soever." I said,"Okay." Ya know I was used to dealing with mobsters so this was nothing new for me with the exception this guy was Irish and not Italian. So he became my manager, and he gave me some money, and we went in the studio and we cut a bunch of songs from that point on. Little did I know he had control of about 32 clubs in Rhode Island, Connecticut, Massachusetts, New Hampshire and Vermont. We started playing his clubs.

The first club we played out of the Triple O's was a place called, "The Cinema Lounge" in Leominster, Massachusetts. We got to the club, and it was a beautiful club in a big strip shopping center. I mean it was gorgeous! All brass and glass. I walked in, and said to the guy behind the bar, "I'm Doc Holiday." He said, "Oh, no problem man." "Set up." So I set up, and I said, "Where's our rooms?" He said, "Go right down the road about 3 miles." "You'll see a big ski lodge on your left hand side." "And just go in there." I said, "OK, cool." I said to the guys, "We're staying in a sky lodge," "How good is this shit?" "Things are looking good with Whitey!" We go down to the ski lodge, and there's nobody in the parking lot. I said, "Well, maybe it's a off day for them?" We go into the lobby, and the front door is open. There's nobody there. Nobody! So I call Whitey up. I said, "Whitey, there's nobody in there." He said, "That's all right." "The place is yours." "Nobody's gonna come in." "It's all yours." Here's this huge ski lodge, and me and my band are staying in it. I said, "Whitey, ya know?" "What do we do about sheets, towels, and stuff like that?" He goes, "Hey, don't worry about it." "Ya just change fuckin' rooms every night." I said, "OK." And that's what we did. We stayed at the ski lodge for 2 weeks, and when the sheets got dirty or when we ran out of towels, we just changed rooms. We had the whole lodge to ourselves. It had like 200 rooms in it, and by the way, there was always a cop car parked outside so nobody could get in but us. Anyway, we continued to work for Whitey for I guess a year and a half to two years. Then all of a sudden, a lot of other stuff started happening in South Boston. It was criminal related. I said, "OK, it's time to get the hell out of here!" Whitey became #1 wanted on the FBI list within 1 month of us bailing out. Later on when Whitey was captured, they made a movie about him starring Johnny Depp called, "Black Mass". It was then that all this other stuff on Whitey came out. They called me for radio interviews from Massachusetts after he was arrested. I did not give them the dirt. (Not like I really knew any to begin with). I said I never saw the bad side of Whitey Bolger. Ya know, it was strictly business. He took care of us, and we made money. We played, but I never seen the dark side of him. Evidently there was a huge dark side. Steve Fleming was accused of assassinating over 100 men. Ya know, but I never got to see that side of them. Whiteys relationship with us was always above board. Whatever he said that's what took place. Ya know.? So anyway, Whitey became legendary in his own right. We moved out, and I decided, "OK, it's time for me to start doing this damn record career." And that's when New York came into effect.

# In Hunt for a Record Deal

Alright, I made up my mind, and figured out it was time to jump back into the recording industry and really pursue my dream of making records. I had already reached what I thought was the epitome of my night club career and being able to perform on stage. It was time to move in the direction that I really got into music for originally and that was to produce and create records.

Only problem was that every record I tried to get someone to let me produce them on, they wouldn't do it because I had no track record doing production. Yeah, I had a track record as an artist because I was performing all over the world, But, not as a record producer. So I scoured the place, all over the industry looking for acts to produce and I couldn't get a shot.

And then it happened, I overdose from Cocain and Heroin in Fort Lauderdale, Florida, I was rushed to the hospital and it was bad, really bad. To be honest with you I don't remember a thing except one thing. I remembered I was laying on a table in the ER Room and I heard my mothers voice, she had rushed down as soon as she heard. I heard her crying and she said to the doctors there "He's all blue" and I heard one of the doctors say "There's a lot of Heroin on board. I blacked out and woke up 5 days later still in the hospital. They had medically detoxed me and I was clean for the first time in 15 years, But I was so weak I could hardly move or speak. I had gone down to 191 pounds in weight. But through that whole ordeal the only thing I remembered was hearing my mothers voice that night in the ER crying. My wife Judy was there when I woke up, she had moved into the hospital and stayed with me 24 hours a day, she never left. I remember telling her to go to the house and gather up all my drug paraphernalia and destroy it all. I had special made mirrors that had groves etched into the glass so you didn't have to scrap the cocain into lines to snort. You just scrapped the coke over the glass and the grooves made its own lines, I had straws to snort the coke made out of 18kt. Gold, 10 mason jars full of black beauty's and enough heroin to kill an elephant. My wife left for the first time since I was admitted and flushed it all down the toilet, smashed the mirrors, broke the needles and threw the gold straws in the ocean.

I stayed in the hospital for 4 weeks and gained 20 pounds. I was released and we moved into a penthouse suite at the Lauderdale Beach Club on the 12th. Floor right on the ocean. I stayed in that bed for about 3 months. My body was totally shot. I could barely walk and my wife brought all my meals up to me from the restaurant in the hotel and I kept gaining weight just laying there. Then one day My mother came by and said, "Butchy you have to get out of that bed, You're killing yourself", so I decided to try and walk out side. It took me 15 mins. Just to walk to the elevator and by the time I got down stairs it took me 30 mins to walk one short block that would have taken a normal person 5 mins to do. My muscles were like mush from laying in bed for so long, but little by little I was coming back, It took me 10 months to get back close to normal, I never lost the weight, I blew up to 280 pounds and that would wind up staying with me all my life, but then I was finally mentally set to get back to my dream so me and my wife moved back to New York City and I was clean and ready to go to work.

I actually started working at a studio called, "Record Plant" a studio in New York as more or less a gopher. Working for producers, getting coffee, pulling the tape out, and everything else, but in a way it was a good thing because I got exposed to major acts that were coming in and I got to see first hand how it was done.

While I was there, Jimi Hendrix came in, and recorded Electric Lady Land and I worked on that. Then there was a group called, Mountain that came in and I was involved with Leslie West, Felix Popalarity, and then the Rascals. So ya know, everything was a plus factor and part of the learning curve for me but, the bottom line was I wanted to produce records but couldn't get a shot. so finally I said, "Oh, the hell with it!" Ya know,, I'll produce me. I knew how to sing, and that's the direction I was forced to take, it was that or nothing.

While I was at the Record Plant, there was an incident when I was in Studio "A" working with an engineer named Jack Adams when one of the receptionists came in and said "Hey John Lennon is in the lobby". Well you know I had to go out there and try to meet him. The lobby of the record plant had a huge wall of this optical illusion thing that was black and white circle graphics off a white background and if you stared at it, it seemed to have the circles moving in and out in motion. They were not really moving, it just seemed that way, it was an optical illusion.

Well I walked into the lobby and there he was The Beatle John Lennon standing in front of the wall just staring at it. I walked up to him and said "Mr. Lennon", he never looked away from the wall but said "Hi Mate", never once looking at me but glued to the wall. I said "I just wanted to tell you I'm a huge fan of your work" once again never looking away from the wall he replied "Thanks Mate and I am of yours". But in reality he really never knew who he was talking to, he never looked away from the wall. So in short that was my first meeting with John Lennon, Later on I would get to be with him once again at Dakota House at a party of sorts and I found him very gracious and by the way I never brought up the first meeting with him.

So I finally recorded an album of all my original songs, and I didn't use the name Doc Holiday. I just used my real last name,"Wahonka." It was all self written stuff, and I started to shop it around New York. I went to 50 or 60 different record labels. At the time, there was a place called the, "The Brill Building. The address was 1650 Broadway. In that building was every record company in the world. I mean they were all there including tons of Publishing companies. I made my record in my spare time when a session I was working on at the plant finished up early and I could grab a few hours of free time When each session was over, and there was an hour or so left over in the studio, I'd go in there and do one of my songs. I wound up playing all the instruments on 90% of the time, but once in a while some of the studio musicians would stay over a bit and help me out and play some of the parts.

I ran it around trying to get a record deal, and I had gone to Roulette Records as one of my stops. While I was at Roulette Records, the president of Roulette was a guy called, Morris Levy. once again, this is when the mobster effect came into the music business. I mean this guy was reputed to be like the Al Capone of the record industry. At the time I had just brushed by him and I never presented him the album. I had met him, and he knew who I was. I didn't present the record to him because he had a guy called, Tim Hardin he was working hard at the time. Tim was actually a folk singer. I think he wrote, "If I were a carpenter?" So he was pretty hot at the time, but he had a lot of demons. He had huge heroin demons. He was tough to handle.

I continued to present the record to ABC, Paramount, Gulf and Western, RCA, Sunbury, Warner, Kama Sutra just to name a few with no luck. Nobody would give me a shot. And finally after about 35 companies turning it down, I had pulled up to the Brill Building one more time as a last ditch effort and I had a friend of mine in the car with me, and I said," Listen, just run this up to Budda." "Ya know, I don't even want to go up there and listen to the rejection." By this time though, I had the thirst for a hit record. I would have done anything for a damn hit. My friend ran the record up. I figured it was just a drop off, and he'd be right back down. So you're in New York right, there's no parking spaces by the Brill Building, and I'm in front of the Brill Building and people blowing their horns trying to get me to move. Jesus Christ I remembered saying, he's taking a half hour, then 45 minutes. I''m saying," What the hell's going on?" Finally he came down, and he said," I sold the album!" I said, "You what?" He said, "I sold the album!"

What had happened was at that time, the record labels had distribution deals with distributors all over the US. In their deals, they would say, "OK, we'll release six new products a year." Or 10 new products. Whatever the number may be. He had just happened to walk into Budda Records at the time when one of their production companies, Super K Productions, had to meet a deadline with one of their distributors, and they needed 10 new albums and only had 9. The order was given, "Whatever comes in, buy it!" "Don't even listen to it." "Just buy it so we can satisfy the distributors." And of course my record was the one that came in. Which goes back to being at the right place at the right time with the right thing and get lucky.

So in short Super K took it, and they said, "OK, we're gonna take it, but we want you to record one of our songs on the album. So I said, "OK." The song was called, Emergency." It was written by, Bobby Blume and Richie Cordell. At the time they were writing all this bubble gum type music that was sweeping the USA. I had signed to the company that had the 1910 Fruit Gum Company, The Ohio Express, and all these bubble gum records and so groups were really hot at that time. They took my album, set up Photo session with a number one photographer at the time "Roger Pollard", I was doing radio interviews, magazine articles, and finally I went into the studio which was The Record Plant once again in New York to record and cut their song that was going to be added to the album "WAHONKA".

Well during that time my album was finally completed with all of my originals and of course with their one song "Emergency" and I remember the day they gave me the recording contract in their offices at 200 west 57$^{th}$, street. The recording contract was probably about 45 pages thick, and I was sitting there with my lawyer. Actually two lawyers, and they (Super K) passed the contract over the desk to me and there was 3 copies of it and it was really thick with pages, and talk about small print? There were tons of it, Christ you needed a magnifying glass to read the God Damn thing, and the lawyers started to peel back the pages one at a time and read it. When I picked up my copy, I peeled all the pages over at once, I just went right to the last page and grab all 40 some pages, flip them over, went to the last page signed it without reading it, and slid it back to them and said, "Just get me the fuckin' hit!" "I want the god damn hit record."

My lawyers said to me, "What the hell are you doing." I said, "That's it!" "Just get me the god damn hit!" And I slid the signed contract back to Super K guys.

So right now, I am finally a signed artist to a major label, and I'm in there with the heavy-weights, I mean these people controlled the top ten on the charts. Not only am I a signed artist, I'm also a signed producer because my album was completed when I gave it to them. But my goal was to get into the machinery of Super K and Budda and I did that at warp speed. I figured out how they were doing this and how they were doing that. It became shocking to know the 1910 Fruit Gum Company and The Ohio Express, those big records like Simon Says, Chewy Chewy, and Yummy Yummy were never actually recorded by those groups. They didn't play on the releases. It was a band from New York called, The Trade Winds. They cut all that stuff. Those bands that were being sold to the public as the artist, and those acts that the public thought were the groups "The 1910 Fruit Gum Company" and "Ohio Express" never played a note one of on those hit records.

I remember I went to a club one night called, "CBGB" with two of the executives from Super K Productions who was also with Budda at the time and there was a band up there playing. I can remember this guy, Hy Gold that worked for Super K and was also with me when I went to the studio to cut Emergency, and he called over the waitress and said to her, "Tell the band leader to come over here." The band leader came over, and Hy said, "Man you sound good!" The band leader said, "I appreciate it man." "Thanks." Then Hy said," How would you like to be in Ohio Express?" The band leader looked at him in amazement. He (the band leader) was not aware that The Ohio Express, Yummy Yummy which was the number one record in the country, was not a real band and they had the #1 record in the country, but they didn't exist. So this band became the Ohio Express. And that was just one time that the public was totally duped.

During that time as well as now the companies as well as the songwriters made money from publishing. Ya know. So if you had the publishing on the song, you made a lot of money. Back then, 45 records were a big thing. So they had this record in the top ten, and there was no record/ song for the flip side. The "B" side. So what they (Super K) did was played the record backwards on one of the Ohio Express records and called it Psychedelic Santa Clause is Coming to Town. It became a song even though it didn't make any sense, sounded like shit, but they collected the publishing royalties off of that song and it was actually on the hit from the "A" side of the record played backwards with a different title.

That was just one of the ways the public was duped thinking these bands existed, and in reality they didn't exist. It was the same band The Trade Winds, that cut all those different hits and recorded them all at Allegro Studios in the Brill Building at 1650 Broadway. They were scamming the public once again 24/7 and the public once again fell for it hook, line and sinker.

And They weren't the only ones doing it. Morris Levy over at Roulette, I mean, it was unreal. He would say to artists "Just shut your mouth, and we'll let you continue to make records." I mean this was strong arm tactics that they were doing just like ya saw with the gangsters on TV. And plus, they had a lock on all the juke boxes at the time. They owned the companies that supplied all the vending machines. They had locked in every possible way of exposure to where they were in total control. I mean they owned it all. It was organized crime at its highest level, but needless to say I got my shot, and I got my album, and I got the song and that's all I cared about.

I can remember that Bobby Blume was signed

to a writing contract with Super K, and somehow he drifted over to Morris Levy's office. Super K wouldn't put a record out on him as an artist, so he went over to Levy and Roulette and they put a record out on him as an artist and the name of the record was, "Montego Bay." It wound up being a top 5 record. Well when the record hit, I went over to Roulette's office with Jeff and Jerry and Hy Gold from Super K and we're sitting in Levy's office . The whole back of his office was all glass. It was like on the 14th floor. You could see the skyline of Manhattan. I remember Jeff or Jerry or one of them said to Morris who was a little small Jewish guy. They said, "Well what are we gonna do?" "This guy Blume is under contract to us as a writer, and we feel we should get a piece of the action of his record you have on Roulette." And this little Jewish guy, Morris Levy stood up, and he said,"Listen Mother Fucker, this is the way this is going down." "You shut ya fuckin' mouth, ya get the fuck out of my office, or ya going through that god damn window, we're gonna make a new fuckin doorway there." And I thought, "Oh shit!" "This is serious shit now!, they shut their mouths quick." and we walked the hell out. Bobby Blume recorded "Montego Bay" for Roulette, and it became a big hit record and Super K got nothing from it.

You need to know that during that time period the record industry in New York was, and as it still is today in that city, a very very fast pace. There is an old saying "Here Today, Gone Tomorrow" well in New York during that time it was "Here Today, Gone Later Today. This was the era of the one hit artist, An artist would pop up with a number one record and then never be heard from again, Hence Here Today, Gone Later Today.

# Cowboy Hats and Boots
## (Big Al Downing, Cissie Lynn, Herman's Hermits, And The Ragin' Cajun, Strange Bed Fellows)

Finally things are starting to go my way. Now I had a record deal. I was in with the movers and the shakers in New York. There was a light at the end of my tunnel, and it was not a roaring train. I was in with major studios, and all I needed to do now was to get into the production world on a first name basis with the heavy weights. This would prove to be one hell of a mountain to climb. That's really what it was all about from day one... getting into that top slot as a producer. It never changed, but now I had the opportunity to slide in because I had a little history behind me in the industry. And, it was all a pretty good history. So I started looking for acts and artists that would let me produce them. By the way, I'm sure I'm gonna miss a couple of them along the way from in the early days.

The first one that came my way was interesting to say the least. It was a guy called, Big Al Downing. He was a black singer out of Oklahoma. I got to know Al real well as a friend. I told Al one one day," Listen, let me produce you." It took a while to convince him, but he finally agreed to it. To be honest with you, I had no experience whatsoever doing country music at that time. My background was in rock & roll. Plus, also at the time, there were no black artist in country music...none! Yeah, a black artist in country music was different alright. However, in every other genre of music, at the time, blacks were having no problem at all. But in country music, blacks were nonexistence. Anyway, to make a long story short, Big Al had a record out called, "Mr. Jones." It was a very big hit in the country field, but he never made any public appearances so the audience never knew he was black. Mainly it was because he sounded like a white singer. Well I finally got with Al, and we were gonna do a continuation of that hit. We were gonna call it, "Mr. Jones The Final Chapter." The only difference this time around was I was going to promote him to the public, and that's where the gamble came him. Not that he was not a tremendous talent, but because of him breaking the mold of a black artist in country music. That wasn't a big deal with me because I had dealt with black artists all my life. There was no color line when it came to talent or really anything else for that matter. But that was the northern way of thinking, and now I'm in the south. Al and I wound up cutting the record in a very small home studio in Hampton, Virginia.

The original story of Mr. Jones was about a sharecropper who adopted a little white boy, and brought him up and raised him like he was his own son. BUT the boy was always in trouble, and would cry out for help saying, "I'm in trouble come and get me Mr. Jones." Mr. Jones would always come running, and get him out of any mess he got into. Well, in the sequel, which was the continuing story of Mr. Jones, the sharecropper's adopted son was in jail at the time of his death. The hook in the first song was, "I'm in trouble." "Come and get me, Mr. Jones." In the sequel Mr. Jones passes away, but the kid is allowed to get out of jail in time for the funeral in handcuffs. The kid shows up at the funeral with the sheriff, and we end the second song while he's standing over the grave of Mr. Jones crying and promising to never again get into trouble. The line went, "I'll never have to say it again." "I'm in trouble." "Come and get me Mr. Jones." We ended it with the same chorus from the first hit. Anyway, we did the record, “Mr. Jones The Final Chapter.” It came out fantastic, and Al was fantastic as he always was. This time he really got into it, and I used every trick I had learned from past productions. The record was a monster.

I brought the finished record to Jim over at Warner Brothers who was president of Warner Brothers Nashville at the time. I said, “Jim, I got this record I want you to listen to.” I didn't tell him it was Big Al. He listen to the record, and said,” Ah man, this is a great record!” I said, “OK, I'm lookin' for a deal with it.” And this was in Nashville when real traditional country music still ruled the roost on music row. This was my first shot in Nashville with major labels, and I needed this to happen. My ass was on the line. Jim said, “Ya gotta picture of him'?” And I said, “Yeah.” He said, “I'd like to see what he looks like?” I said, “Ok.” And I gave him a promotional picture of AL. He looked at me, and scratched his head and said,” Doc! “I said, “What?” He said, “He's black!!!,” I said, “Yeah, I noticed that, but they can't tell that on the radio.” Cause, ya know, he sounds white. He said, “I don't know, man.” “Country music, I don't know if they're ready for a major black artist?” I said, “Jim, I just need a shot here.” “This is a great record.” “You know it's a great record.” “Nobody is gonna know he's black, and probably won't give a shit?” “They're gonna buy the record.” Deep inside of me I knew

I was gonna push Al out there to the public, and trust me, the country music fans were gonna know this is a black artist.

Anyway, in the end after a little brow beating, I got a shot with the record. The record was huge! Big Al became huge! I started to produce a lot of stuff on him. I probably produced 18 or 20 songs on him. I got him some major television shots, and he was also touring all over the country. A television talk show at the time called, Nashville Now, which was hosted by an ex DJ name Ralph Emory, took a huge liking to Big Al. He had him on that show all the time.

I'm gonna jump ahead at this point. Later on, I get Al a tour in Canada. Actually, his first Canadian tour. His record was huge in Canada, so this was a slam dunk for him. He was always, no matter what he did... broke. He was constantly broke even though he was making huge amounts of money. The man had no idea how to manage his money. His lifestyle just completely blew him out of cash. So, he was always in bad financial shape. I booked him I think 8 concert dates in a row in Canada at $7,500.00 a show which was pretty good damn money back then. And I said, "OK, here's the dates Al." "Ya just go up and do the deal, and make some damn money." He didn't have to travel with a band because the promoter up there was supplying the band free of charge. They had a band there that had rehearsed all of Al's songs. Plus his rooms were all paid for as well as all his meals . He just had to get in there, sing his songs, and come out with over 50 grand in 8 days.

So, he took the dates because he needed the money. And I said, "OK, your first stop is Moncton, New Brunswick, Canada and it's called "The Urban Cowboy." He was supposed to open there on a Friday night. Al lived in Massachusetts at the time. So as usual, he leaves the last damn second on Thursday morning. He leaves to drive to Canada! About 4:00 pm on Friday afternoon, I get a call. It's Al, and it's a collect call. Go figure. He's in Calais, Maine. He's stuck at the Canada-Maine border. I answered the phone and said, "Yeah Al" "What's up?" He said, "I can't get into the country." I said, "What the fuck do you mean you can't get into the country?" "We filled all the paperwork out" "Everything's fine!" He said, "Na, I need $75. 00 to get into the country." I said, "Al, you don't have $75.00 on you?" He said, "No!" I said, "How the hell are you going out of the country for 8 show dates, with no money in your pocket?"

So anyway, I had to find a place to wire him money at the border to get him into the country. Seventy-five dollars so he could get into Canada. It's just a little funny story on Big Al Downing, and it continued on that way throughout his whole career. I mean he was constantly never able to get ahead. He wound up having many hit records, doing many television appearances, and was well known in country music. It was good for Al, and it was also good for me.

Now, before I know it, I'm head long into country music. And,ya know, I 'm a rocker from New Jersey and New York. I came from pop, bubblegum, and R&B background. The next thing you know, I'm in Nashville wearing a goddamn cowboy hat and boots. So, along comes this girl, Cissie Lynn. What makes her different from the thousands of other female singers in Nashville trying to make it, is she is the daughter of the iconic country singer Loretta Lynn. She wants to sing or as she says it, "I Wanna Be A Sanger". I will say this, she is one beautiful girl! I mean just gorgeous looking, and she can sing her ass off. If anybody sounded like Loretta, it was her. In my personal opinion, Cissie was better than her mama. Loretta was promoting all her children except Cissie. I couldn't figure it out cause all the other children to be honest with you, sucked compared to Cissie. Cissie was the real deal singer of all the other off springs. She was the dead wringer for Loretta Lynn's voice and style.

So, I got together with her and I said, "Listen, we're gonna put you a band together, and we're gonna put you out on the road and we're gonna cut one record on you to test it out and see if the public and radio will dig what your doing."

She agreed to it. We cut it and she put her whole heart into it, but she was married to this moron at the time name John. He was a real fuckin' asshole! I mean he was nothing but a Loretta Lynn groupie. I mean he didn't marry Cissie Lynn. He married Loretta Lynn's daughter. He had no idea who Cissie was, but she fell for his bullshit. He was a thorn in her side throughout her whole career, and finally totally destroyed her personally and professionally. I mean, every time she made a move, it went sour. and She couldn't figure out why it went sour. It was totally because of him behind the scenes. I always told her, "Lynn Kid, love is blind, BUT IT AINT STUPID!"

Anyway, I put her on the road with a bunch of show dates, and naturally he had to go along as "The Band Leader". Yup, he's the band leader alright...or so he claimed to be. He couldn't play his way out of a paper bag, but he's the band leader and he's on stage with her every goddamn night. Well before she opens with her first job, she's living at the time (this will kill ya) in a run down, beat up single wide trailer. This is Loretta Lynn's daughter living in a run down beat up trailer eating spam. Loretta's living in this big mansion in Hurricane Mills "The Loretta Lynn Dude Ranch." Okay, so we take her the hell out of there, and put her on the road. She scores big time! Big time! Every place she plays, she knocks em dead! People are lovin' this girl, and she's pulling in fans like crazy. She's starting to make some decent money for the first time in her life. I gave her the name. CISSIE LYNN ," The Daughter of the Coal Miner's Daughter." Later on, while on a television talk show after Cissie had started to make it, Loretta claimed she came up with the name. Which she was, after all, Loretta's daughter. Loretta's band was called, "The Coal Miner's." I called Cissy's band, "The Coal Dusters." She's doing great , and she's making money. Everything is good. The fans are loving her.

I booked her into Canada to do an eight week tour, and as soon as she crossed the border, we get the threat of a law suit! It was from none other than Loretta's manager at the time! There gonna sue Cissy for using the name The Coal Dusters. It was too much like The Coal Miner's which was Loretta's band. I said, "I can't believe this horse shit!" "The mother is gonna sue her kid!" Of all the other siblings that she's promoting, and got on the road with her while doing nothing for Cissie, she's gonna sue her? So I said to them, "Just bring it the fuck on!" "All right!" "We'll grind them into the goddamn ground!" And we did! I mean, we backed them off big time.

Cissie did the Canadian tour, and went back to Hurricane Mills. The first thing she did was buy an elaborate double wide trailer. I mean it was beautiful. It was gorgeous! She had money; she had a new car, and everything else that went along with it! Everything was great! And she was doing great. Her future looked even greater. She was making great recordings, and the fans were loving her. We got this songwriter named Terry Maretti, and he wrote a song for her titled, "I'm the Daughter of the Coal Miner's Daughter." We were gonna launch it with a ton of promotion money behind it. Everything was good, but now here comes the problem. Husband, John, who is not really a husband of any sort! The guy was a piece of shit! He was as I said from the start, a Loretta Lynn groupie. That's all he ever was.

Anyway, he steps in and he goes," Well, we don't want you to manage us anymore." Cissie isn't saying that! John is saying that. He said, "Ah, I think I can do a better job." So I said, "Hey, you do what ya gotta do!" "It don't make no difference to me!" "I've got bigger fish to fry!"

And, he took over. From day one when he took over, just to tell ya, at the end he drove her into bankruptcy. OK, we had her doing great. He drove her into bankruptcy, and she was dead broke. Finally, I'm gonna jump ahead...way ahead. She finally got smart years later, and divorced his ass! But now, by the time she got smart, she was too old to start over again. Her health was going bad, and she wasted the best years of her life on that piece of garbage! Anyway, sad as it may sounds, that's the REAL Cissie Lynn story.

So now I'm in Nashville, I'm in country

music, and everything is going great. Well, from out of left field, I get a call from the drummer of Herman's Hermits, Barry, in London, England. He's wanting me to produce them. I jumped at the shot. I mean I grew up listening to Herman's Hermits, and here it is I get to produce them. I brought them over to Virginia from England, and we do an album on the Hermits. The group at the time did not contain Peter Noone the original singer, but a guy called Keith Roberts, who in my opinion, was 100 times better than Peter. Well, the Hermits were in the studio setting up their instruments, and a funny thing happened.

There was a newspaper reporter from the Washington Post there doing a story on them. The Washington Post for those of you that don't know was a big east coast newspaper. Their crew came in with both cameras and videos cameras. One of the newspaper reporters said, "Doc, ya mind if we take a bunch of footage and still pictures while they're recording?" I said, "No, feel free!" As they're interviewing them, one guy said, "Listen, why don't you guys like play us a song, ya know, and we'll use that as a backdrop." So I said, "Yeah!" "Cool!" "Let's do it!" So, I had everything turned on, and all of a sudden they went, "Deed da la dunt dunt da dunt." Ya know? They started playing this song. It was, "Mrs. Brown You've Got a Lovely Daughter." When they did it, it was exactly like the original record, and I was blown away! They had this guy Keith Roberts that had taken Peter Noone's place, and he sounded exactly like the original record! It was awesome that I was sitting there listening to this record that I grew up on!

The Herman's Hermits record was finally released, and I made a lot of money with it. The Hermits themselves started touring, and they did very well. I'm on my way again. I mean, I can't make a mistake! Everything I touch is turning into gold! So before ya know it, I'm saying, "OK, I'm good to go here!" Everything is perfect!" "I'm producing records like I wanted to, I'm with the right people, and the best is I'm producing hit records, and I'm getting known in the industry."

Then, in my life comes "The Ragin' Cajun" Doug Kershaw. A Brilliant entertainer, and a well deserve reciprocate of the term "Living Legend." Doug came to me with a duet, a song titled, Cajun Baby. It featured a young untested, as far as the entertainment industry was concerned, singer by the name of Hank Williams Jr.. The duet was brilliant to say the least. It was perfect marriage of the legendary Cajun sound with an angry young man that would become known throughout the world as an outlaw country singer. The record was a smash around the world, and added another notch in the gun of Doug Kershaw. Also it was for sure, a big notch in my personal gun in the industry. I went on to produce Doug

Kershaw over the next 25 years, and through it all I became a huge fan of Doug and his incredible talent. But more so, I gained a very intimate friend who as an artist and a person, I will respect as long as I am on this earth.

# Close But No Cigar
## (The Hit's and The Misses)

OK, right now my career as a producer is just flat out fantastic. I'm mean I producing a lot of big names. I'm getting to work in big major multi million dollar recording studios, and it's to the point where I'm starting to get world wide recognition as a producer. And from out of nowhere I get this brilliant idea. I see a lot of new artists out there, and they just can't get into the major highway of the entertainment business. So once again I get this brilliant idea of doing untested artists for a budget price and then releasing them worldwide to radio and also distributing them on every major download site. Ya know just a song or two, and giving them a shot in a major way with radio and distributing their record. Once I started this there was a constant supply of new artists coming from all over the world.

I'm gonna run down just a few of them. Ya know some of em' that got so close to clicking big time, and just missed the boat for one reason or another. Because there are a lot of different things that have to fit into the equation in order to become a hit recording artist. It's not just being able to sing or write a song. You have to have the right financial backing that can support you in this industry to get started, because this industry today is all about money, and the rates to do all of the above correctly are outrageous. And if you're using the right musicians, they cost you a lot of money. And the right studios, they cost you a ton of money. Those studios aren't doing it for free.

I hear artists all the time say, "Well if I'm that good, I shouldn't have to pay!" Well all ya have to do is convince that studio to do it for free, and these musicians who have worked all their lives to build up the resumes to do it for free. And then take the producer and say, "OK, you worked all your life to get a reputation and to know your trade, and you gotta work for free. JUST BECAUSE I'M GOOD!!!" It's not gonna happen. It's never gonna happen. Everyone on the original recordings, ya know when ya first go in, the burden of proof and financial input is in the artist's lap. Period. Or it's in somebodies lap that they happen to know very well, VERY WELL.

Somebody has to put the money up. Period, Before anything can happen. And most major labels want to see a track record and a huge fan base on an artist before you can even be considered. They wanna see a strong past performance record. Labels aren't gonna take a chance. They are not in a business of gambling. If they were they'd go to a casino, and put a million dollars down on black or red on a roulette wheel. So in short get that idea of "I'm a great singer and I wrote a great song and look how good I look, IT DON'T MEAN SHIT!!!!! It's all about you proving to them (the labels, the agents) you can make them money!!!!!

So anyway, to get on with the program. I got this brilliant idea of doing a series of albums called breakout artists. So we just put up a post announcing the project on social network saying, "OK, we're gonna give these new artists a major shot." And, we did that! And some of them like I said, were so great man!

There was a guy named, Brody. He came into QUAD Studios and the guy was phenomenal! I mean, he wrote songs and sang the hell out of them, and to say he was GREAT is an understatement. When he came to Nashville, we recorded him at Quad Studios a 12 million dollar plus studio on Music Row. One of the premier recording studios. And we went all in using my studio A Team which features a lot of Hall of Fame musicians.

Brody came in, and he sang this song and just blew everybody away. While he was in town, "HE" got an offer from Nickelodeon the TV show. They were gonna take him, and do some things with him on the television station that Nickelodeon controlled. Well, everything was going great, and I just said, "Ya know this kid is gonna make it." And I can remember Mark, who was the manager of Quad Studio plus he was also the base player for Garth Brooks, and he came in and said, "Doc, this kid is ready now!" And we all believed it.

Well, I get a call from Brody. probably five weeks after we're into the project. He said, "Doc, I have to tell you something." I said, "Yeah Brody, shoot!" And he goes, "Ummm, I was born a woman." And I said, "What!" I mean because he looked as male, and acted as male as any male I had ever seen. And he said, "I'm having an operation that's changing me to a male." And he had to go over in some third world country to get this operation that would take over a period of a year and the cost was through the roof. I said, "Well ya know, that's cool." "Ya know, I'm here to support ya." "Everything is cool." "You're phenomenal, and I back you 100%" And I got to really like Brody as not only a super talented artist but also a great human being.

But what happened was Brody started to promote that transformation of being born a girl, and changing to a male on the internet and on television. Unfortunately, at the time, (things are different today) but at the time, that was taboo. I mean it was total taboo to country fans anyway. And it more or less killed his career. That was a shame because he was phenomenal! I mean just a brilliant, brilliant artist! And still is a brilliant artist today. And maybe he'll resurface again today because society has now become more attune to accepting that whole situation.

That was one of the artists. There were other ones. I remember there was this couple from Florida. The husband proclaimed himself a songwriter, and I will say he did write some pretty damn good songs. However, he was all over the place. One was a disco song, one was blues song, one was a love song. And you can't do that. Ya gotta say, "Listen, this is the direction I'm going in, and this is what I gotta write. Well in short he was writing the songs, and the wife was singing them. She had a unique voice, and in this business I've always said, "You don't have to be good." "You have to be different." And that's the key. That's the key to success. Being different. Take for instance Johnny Cash. Nobody sings like Johnny Cash. And you know, Bob Dylan, sure as hell ain't never gonna go in a singer's Hall of Fame, but he's still Bob Dylan. He's different. So that's the key. She was and still is a GREAT singer, BUT remember she was also very different sounding. She had a real innocent angelic type voice. The only problem was the husbands material that he was writing for her, (and she would only record his material), some of it was right on the money, but most of it was way the hell out in left field some place. And therefore, she was spread thin vocally and it was like, "Where do you put this record in the record store?" "Under what category?" "Do you put it under country?" "Do you put it under blues? "Do you put it ???? You can't do that to a singer." Ya can't spread them thin like that. You gotta give them room to express themselves, Ya gotta stick to certain sound and direction that fits their natural ability, not try and force them into a pocket that they can't be themselves. Ya know when the Rolling Stones play a song, ya don't have to know it's the Rolling Stones, ya know it just by listening and hearing that trademark sound of theirs. And that was the problem with her. She was tremendous, had a tremendously different voice and different application of putting it into a lyric. But the husband, (and I love him to death as a person and a talent), I honestly love them both, they're great people BUT THIS IS BUSINESS FOLKS. He screwed her career up by not focusing in one direction and also killed it by trying to lead the way in every position, he pictured himself as a producer, video director, song writer, manager, you name it. He did everything after he left the studio with me, his way. And it wasn't like I didn't tell him. "Ya gotta pinpoint her, and set her in a direction." Her natural direction is front porch music ya know?" Sitting on the front porch with banjos and that Americana feel and that kinda thing.

She had one folk type song that was a smash on radio and the New Music Weekly, STS Radio charts. Ya know, that's where ya need to focus her in that direction. And ya know, he just didn't listen. And in the mean time... She started out great. Her first 2 records went top 10 on the New Music Weekly charts. I mean she was right on the money. And then he just decided, "Hey, I'm gonna go in this direction, and released a Disco type song. It destroyed her. Then he even produced a half ass video on that song that threw out a whole different image of what she really was and what her radio public perceived her to be. He would not listen to me, and bring her back in the path where radio liked her. In the end he submitted a few songs to me and they were both duets with him and her, I strongly suggested she record some songs also that were written by other writers that fit her like a glove, it was then that I realized that he did not take the career serious and was treating it more as a hobby so I passed on doing anything with them again. To me this is not a hobby it's serious business and if you're not in it to make the score then it's time for me to walk away.

And, ya know, there was also a guy called Paul, who probably was one of the best folk singers that I ever recorded in my entire career. The only problem with him was when he sang, (It really wasn't a problem) he sounded exactly like Gordon Lightfoot. But, his appearance was different enough to make him different. And at the time Gordon wasn't releasing a lot of records so there was a huge gap in the market place. People were still wanting and looking for that type of music, and he fit it like a glove. The only problem was he didn't want to do that. He was an older gentleman in his 60's with a big long white beard, and he was trying to sing, ya know, new country type songs, and it just didn't fit. And I kept putting him in that Gordon Lightfoot bag, and he kept forcing his way out of it to do what he wanted to do. So to make a long story short, he auditioned for a well known television talent show. And he called me up and he said, "What should I sing?" I said listen," Sing Early Morning Rain." "or sing a Gordon Lightfoot signature song. And you'll kill, you'll kill doing it, Trust me you will knock it out of the park." Well, he didn't listen to me. He went on there and he sang some kind of new country bullshit thing, and it bombed BIG TIME. He claimed to me when I asked him why he did that song, he said the producers made him sing that song (rather than the one I told him to sing) which I found out later after talking to two of the producers of the show was a little bit of a fib, because the producers will let you sing whatever you wanted to sing in the auditions and long story short he didn't get one vote, NOT ONE DAMN VOTE FOR ONE HELL OF A FOLK SINGER. OK, so you put that behind you, and you figure out what went wrong. You say to yourself, I'm taking the wrong route here, and you go back to what you were doing. Instead, he publicizes that failure on social network. Facebook and so on and so on... of failing. And saying, "I ain't done yet!" THE FUCK YOU AIN'T, Ya don't publicize a national television failure. Ya know, ya publicize winning. Ya learn from failure. You don't publicize it. And that was the end of his recording career. And it's a shame because he was and probably still is brilliant at doing Gordon Lightfoot type Folk material.

Then there was another artist, I know I'm going on and on here But it's important to note, and name as many as I can of these new artists, and how they almost made it. They almost got to the finish line, but for some reason, they blew it. Ya know, there's a lot of reasons that they blew it. It was never the production, it was never the music, it was never the songs. It was because of something else that came into the equation, and busted it up.

Another guy came from Maine. He was a singer songwriter. Probably about 60 years old which is too old for the industry or so they say, but he looked extremely good for his age, very hip looking, and the material (songs) he was singing and writing related to that older age bracket. He was an excellent song writer. I mean he wrote comedic type stuff, he wrote fun stuff, he wrote everything that was entertaining. The only problem was he had a controlling wife who kind of interfered with everything and just wouldn't let him pursue it. Ya know, he did an album. He had a lot of success on it, and he had a lot of energy to self promote his project. He was hitting the self promotion hard, and then he just stopped. Ya can't stop. Ya gotta finish the race. Period. And he never finished it, and to this day He's playing open mike nights doing absolutely nothing on a major level, BUT guess what? his wife is now singing with him OK, So, it's a different ballgame completely. With all due respect to her, she doesn't sing very well in my opinion, but she is a very gracious woman. She sure as hell can't write a song very well. And he had all those things captured. So, at the end, as close as he got to getting it, something else came in from left field, not music related, and stopped his progress.

There were many of them. Oh yea, there was a girl called, Zing, who was fantastic, but recorded two songs, only two songs that were GREAT, but never followed through. One more called Mike. Mike was a preacher who did one song with me and he was smooth as butter and had a strong shot at an older market. But once again never followed through with more recordings. Then came a guy Samuel. He had a different style completely but because of personal reasons (a girlfriend and her family that was bleeding him dry of money) he did not continue the path and was left with wondering, "what if?". But he had a strong shot at making it.

Another one, Robin. Unbelievable blues singer and writer. And what she did was, she recorded one record, one song with us, it came out great and the next thing ya know she going to this budget bullshit Nashville studio and producer where they record the music for you, while you're sitting at home and you do the singing and you send them the vocal track. Just a typical Nashville ripoff. And it's all cookie cutter music. But, she was phenomenal. Another girl was Terry. Unbelievable voice! Ya know, these are all middle age women. And Terry, ya know, the same thing. Recorded one record, one song, but for some reason unable to continue the journey to make it happen. But every single one of them had a decent shot to get it done, and for some reason something came out of left field that was not musically related most of the time and stopped them cold.

Then came a kid from North Dakota. When he was first brought to me for the possible recording, my first thought was to turn him down. I mean the kid sounded like shit, he was hitting these choir boy sounds, trying to sing as high as he could sounding like a strangled bird that had his balls in a vice grip, and the songs he was writing were the same damn 4 chords over and over, plus he looked like shit, short hair, big ears and dressed like some flea market poster child. BUT I agreed to meet with him rather than make a judgment call shooting from the hip and as a favor to the guy that "discovered" him, Johnny Green. Johnny pushed me pretty hard to meet with this kid.

Now that meeting was a shocker, this kid had no personality at all, he was like a robot, no emotions what so ever. He didn't laugh, hell he didn't even smile and when he spoke it was like listening to a robot computer voice. BUT when I listened to him sing, once in a while I heard some magic in that voice in a line or the way he would phrase a certain line. So I thought I need to find out what has happened to this kid to make him like he was and just maybe I could get that magic I heard in a few lines he sang out. So he flew out to me from North Dakota and drove down to Nashville with me. I figured 14 hours in a car and I would get to what made this kid like he was and maybe unlock that talent that was hidden in there.

I can remember asking him in the car on the drive down to Nashville, "So what the fuck happened to you?, he looked at me and said "what do you mean?, "I said your a fuckin vegetable man". Well it took maybe 8 hours of talking and he started to loosen up and tell me about how he was being raised and all the bullshit that was being placed on him. Than it all started to come together and make sense why this kid was so fucked up. An unbelievable controlling mother was the route of the whole problem. The stories he told me about her would fill a whole other book. Forcing him to go to church, how to dress, how to wear his hair. Shit he told me when he lost his virginity, she found out and went fucking ballistic, it was like the end of the world, she actually made him go to church and pray to Jesus for forgiveness and mind you he was an adult and wore a fuckin' rubber when he did it.

Anyway enough about her, the damage was already done to this kid, this was child and mental abuse at it's highest level. BUT the good thing was he was willing to come out of his shell and fix everything. So I set on the journey of bringing this kid back into the real world, and the best was he was willing to learn, and like I said there was still magic in that voice, I just needed for him to let it out and not do things like his mother wanted but do things that HE wanted. I had to convince him that at age 20, HE was in control of his life NOT HER!. I showed him how to buy clothes that someone in the entertainment business would wear, fix his hair the way he wanted it to be not the way she wanted it to be, grow a little facial hair so he didn't look like a little goofy school kid, and then I started to teach him a bit about how to write and sing a song "The right way".

The kid was like a sponge, he took it all in and that magic started to come out and when it did, it was like the talent flood gates opened up, he was and is fuckin awesome!!! and today as of the writing of this book he has won numerous music awards, had 5 charted TOP TEN records, and has 3 albums entered into the GRAMMY AWARDS plus had his music played on radio in 43 countries around the world, HE is on his way, which only proves I was right, right from the git go, if you do everything I say and do everything I say to do career wise, I WILL GET YOU THERE!!! It only took me 60 years to learn how this business works (smile) Oh the mother?? She is still there trying to control every step of the way, Only difference is, NOW the young man totally ignores her AND SO DID I. BUT sad to say she wore him down and now, he is sitting there with her in control and I walked away from it.

I could go on like this forever, but these good artists deserve mentioning in this book. Ya know, they were that good. They had the talent, but they just didn't fit the mode of where the music industry was headed. Ya know, they wanted those young kids. Nineteen years old...twenty years old that look like models. They really didn't care if they could sing or not. Just as long as they had that appearance. We went through some really good acts man that were strong. I mean really strong, and should have been there. Ah but like I've always said before, unmusical related problems always popped up, and stopped them cold.

It's the way it is but, then I also have to hit on some of the ones who were, well lets just say shouldn't have been there to begin with. Not that they weren't talented now. They were all talented other wise I would have never agreed to record them in the first place, but their heads were up their fuckin' asses.

I mean you couldn't tell them anything. They swore to God they had all the answers. And it's simple. If ya got all the answers, and ya know what it's supposed to sound and be like, why the fuck are you coming to me to begin with? if you're not gonna listen to what I say, why ya coming to me to begin with? And all of the time I never found this out until we were in the studio recording them.

One of em' was this guy Stephan. This guy swore to God he was the next Garth Brooks. He came in, and his ego was bigger than the building at Sony studios. Ya know? And I tried to say, "Listen do it this way, or do it that way, Forget about it! Ya know it was like talking to a brick wall, "He told me, This is what I want, this is the way it should sound!" "Period, end of sentence." And finally, it just missed the boat completely, and actually later on he did do it himself and it REALLY fuckin' bombed! I mean so here's a guy, that finally wound up paying his own money to do it his way and he fell flat on his ass?

And there were other ones. Um, another one was this guy Dalton. Whoa, this guy was from left field, outter space. All right? He came in, he wanted this, he wanted that, he wanted this... He wanted to spend four days in the vocal booth to sing a 4 min. song that he had written, and do this and do that. The guy was a complete idiot when it came to producing a record. And then when we came back to him, and said, "Listen, this is the way it's gotta go." "We've already tested this." "We did a video on it." The video gathered 3000 views immediately. Ya know, 3000 plus views I might add. And his other videos that he did himself had like 100, to 150 views. It didn't make any difference. This guy came back to us and said. Ya know, ah, "Dalton and team want it this way." Well "Dalton and team" fell flat on their asses, and now he's working in some dump in Gatlinburg TN.. Ya know, still thinking that he's the next Tim McGraw. Oh By the way we later found out there never was a Dalton and his team it was all a figment of his imagination.

Another was this guy Jason. Great singer. Great writer. Had it all going for him, but ya know when they just miss the boat for some reason or another, they don't blame themselves, they blame the producer, or they blame the production, or they blame the studio, or they blame the players. And in fact, they're the ones who are at fault. Ya know, that list of just missing the boat, goes on and on and on, and it's their own damn fault. It 's their own fault completely! But, in between all that bullshit, there were those good ones that came through that did miss because of nothing that they did what so ever, and missed the boat because of non musical things.

Ya know, I have to mentioned a guy named Jim. He did a song called, "Southern Sunday Morning." The guy was and still is phenomenal! But, he was too old for the God damn industry standards. And then this guy T-bone. I mean, great, raw Americana artist, man once again too old. Ya know, he was too old for the industry and where the major labels were headed.

There were so many, I could go on for ever, and this chapter would be a book in itself. Ah, but, ya know, it is what it is. And, I know that every time we went into the studio, ever single time no matter where it was, we pulled all the stops out. Every possible thing we could do, we did 110%. There was a kid from I think it was Colorado. Fabulous writer. Fabulous singer. His name was Paul. And he was right there. He was right there locked and loaded ready to go. Ready to fire, but he met a girl, fell in love. And the girl told him, "Well I don't want you to do this. I want to settle down , buy a house and be ":Normal" So He quits! He just stopped! Ya know, it's bullshit like that that killed him and many others in this business. Um, there was a girl too, April. Ok? Everything was fine with her. Ya know, she sang. And she was actually, at one time, in a session singing the wrong note. It Was flat at hell. Wasn't even close to the right note! And finally after five or six times, I got on the board mic and I said, "Ah excuse me." "You do know that you're singing the wrong note right?" And she tried it another six times, and continued to do the wrong note. We finally got her just to sing one note, we pitch corrected it and we cut and pasted it in to make it fit. Well at the end, she just thought she didn't know why she wasn't getting Lexus and Rolls Royce pulling in her driveway after recording one song. We wound up actually, for the first time (and last time), giving this broad her money back just to get rid of her. I mean that's how "out to lunch" she was.

Ya know, it just goes on and on. Like I said, this chapter could be a book in itself, but it is what it is. But always in between that stream of bullshit make believe wannabe artists, there were the good artists. There was the artist like Jim Boyd. Ya know, who did songs that were scary man that they were so good. This guy was an eight time Nammy (Native American Music Award) winner! Ya know? He was a pro. He went in there, and he got it done. But I learned real quick that dream that I had of giving these young artists a shot at major stuff was not a good idea. It was for some of them, but for some of them, they were just pain in the asses and didn't deserve to be there to begin with. So, it kinda tells ya, if they're not there, well maybe they didn't belong there to begin with? So, I just scrubbed that whole idea, and we went on.

# The Nashville Hustle

Well I discovered one thing. The farther I got into the music industry in Nashville, the more I realized how corrupt, crooked, and what a con game it was, Not all of it, but a big part of it. Now, I' m not talking about the major artists. I'm talking about the vanity labels, and independent recording artists. There are hundreds of them out there pouring into Nashville everyday. An endless stream of wannabe stars. There are different, little small record labels that offer services to young stars who are coming to Nashville and want to record in Nashville and make it to the "Big Time". And these Gooberville con men usually bring them into these small bull shit computer driven studios with the same session players making the rounds in the "Music City". They're all cookie cutters? They just knock the stuff out sounding all the same. It's not major label quality, not even close, but in their brain these vanity labels are doing to the artist what the artist thinks, "Hey, I'm a big recording star in Nashville!"

To prove that point, they create these make believe radio/record charts that have you at number 2, and Waylon Jennings is at number 4. Or, you're at number 3, and Johnny Cash is at number 6. And you think," Hey, I'm beating Johnny Cash!" "I'm beating Waylon Jennings," In realty, your not beating anybody! It's a fake chart it's all bullshit! It has no bearing what so ever on the reality of what is really happening! It's created and done just to take these artists money. And most of these vanity labels/studios have a flat fee for their so called services. One song for around $1,200.00, and we'll promote it for another $2,000.00, (actually they are all different fees, BUT it's still the same bullshit).

And once you have recorded and what they called "Released" you get to ride the "HILLBILLY CON TRAIN" you'll get these fake chart numbers and a few radio reports from radio stations that have a listening audience of like 10 people in the middle of Butt Fuck North Dakota. At the end of the day, you think you're a big star, and you go down to the corner mention your name to somebody, and nobody knows who the fuck you are! I personally look at these charts sometimes, and

I see all these artists names, and I say, "Who the hell are these fuckin' people?" Where do they come from? And it goes on and on and on and it was like that in Nashville 40 years ago and it's still like that now today. These vanity labels are still doing the same bullshit over and over and getting away with it.

I'll tell you a true story. I recorded an artist called Richie Balin. He was a phenomenal artist and still performing today. We went out, and we popped the first record on him, and it made it to Billboard. It reached like number 50 on Billboard (by the way) Billboard is a solid legitimate chart. The artist (Richie) was really great and deserved to be there and even higher on that chart. The second record on him came out was number 45 on Billboard (So he's on the move in the industry and he's touring doing live shows, A big Plus factor). The Third record was released, and there was a promo team in Nashville that was headed by a guy known as Chuck D. that we decided to do some extra promotion on this release.

So in short Chuck D. wound up as one of the promo teams on the Richie Balin third release. The Billboard promo was not done by Chuck D. Chuck handled the chart in Cashbox Magazine, Billboard Magazine charts was promoted by a guy name Gene Kennedy. Gene Kennedy was legit across the board. Chuck D. was nothing but a god damn con man and a thief. He (Chuck) called me to come in his office and he said, "Listen, I just debuted him at number 80 on this chart that was Cashbox." Not Billboard, but Cashbox "Can I get a bonus for bringing him in so high". And I'm sitting in his office and I said," Ah 80 debut." "That's pretty damn good ya know!" "This is Richie's third record, and he debuts at 80." And while I'm talking to Chuck D., I look on the floor in the corner of his office and there's a stack of 45 records there. I reach down and I picked up one of the records, and it's Richie's record! It hasn't even been shipped to radio! No Cashbox radio stations that were reporting had the record, but yet they're showing it at number 80 on the charts with these fake ass radio station reports that show they are supposedly playing it. At that point I said, "This is a bunch of horseshit!, and you want a fuckin bonus???"

Now with the Cashbox charts they (Chuck D. and his crew) are controlling the back 50. So, In other words, any place in from number 50 to 100 on the chart they can put the records wherever they want, even though they're not getting played any place. Now here is the greatest unspoken con ever in "Music City". Up pops a new organization called SESAC. There was BMI, and there was ASCAP, and there was also now SESAC. These were all primary publishing and songwriter organization/unions that are use to make sure the songwriters and publishers get paid when somebody uses their music. But In order for SESAC to make it's headway into the publishing game, they said, "We are not gonna scan or pay according to actual radio plays or sales." "We are not gonna pay by radio plays." "We're not gonna scan radio stations." "We're gonna pay for chart position." "If the record gets into the 90's, we'll pay $3,000.00 to the writers and publishers." "If it get's into the 80's, we'll pay another $3,000.00." "Into the 70's, we'll pay another $3,000.00." "into the 60's, we'll pay another 3,000.00." So do the math, that's 12 grand if your record is in the 60's. Unbeknownst to SESAC, these Nashville promotion guys are totally controlling the back 50! From 50 to 100 and I might add all under the watchful eye of the publisher and owner of Cashbox, George Albert, they're putting records wherever and whenever they wanted. So what they do is they take a record, and they'll go to Cashbox and they'll say, "Ok, we need this record at # 92. The guy will say, "I need some radio reports." They'll do what they call paper ads. There is no radio station actually playing it, there is no spins, there is no plays. Paper ads are all fake reports most of them filled out by the program directors or DJ's on these small stations who were usually on the take from these Promo guys, (NOT ALL OF THEM BUT MOST). They'll bring the records in at number 90, grab $3,000.00 from

SESAC, and next week they'll move it to number 82, grab another 3 grand. The next week they'll move it into the 70's. Grab another 3 grand. Next week, move it into the 60's and grab another 3 grand and the next week it will drop out of the charts. It's gone. It's history. It's up, and then out. I mean, it doesn't even like creep it's way down. It just goes out of the charts. And, ya know ya say, "12 grand, well that ain't a lot of money." They're working 10 records a week. They're making $120,000.00 a week off of SESAC ALONE!!!! just by manipulating the charts.

Well, low and behold Cashbox hires a new guy to do their charts. His name is Kevin Hughes. Kevin Hughes is a young kid, Sharp kid. He sees that the charts are being manipulated by Chuck D. and his crew and He makes an announcement to Chuck D., "Listen, this fuckin' bullshit ain't gonna keep going on." "I need to have legitimate radio charts." "Otherwise, I'm not gonna do this number game you guys are pullin'." Well they argued with him, and of course you're taking a lot of money from these guys, but Kevin stuck to his guns. He said, "I'm not gonna do it." "Either they are legitimate radio charts, or I 'm not gonna do it." Sadly, a week later, Kevin Hughes was shot in Music Row at broad daylight. No one was ever brought to trial on it or convicted of the crime.

Now I can't prove it, but I'm telling you

right now it was because of those charts. You hit somebody for $120,000.00 a week, your life is worthless when it comes to this kind of organized crime. Especially when you're dealing with scum like that.

Now Chuck and his crew are in trouble at Cashbox. The heat is really on them. They can't chart their records, and SESAC gets smart. They said, "OK, we're not doing this bullshit anymore." "We're gonna start scanning radio plays and sales" so now that little hustle they had going is gone or at least for the SESAC side of it. BUT, they still have these young artists all coming to Nashville to be big superstars. So, they need a chart that they can control. And there's a magazine in Texas called, The Indie Bullet ran by a guy called Roy Hause, Jason H., and Gary B. is the promo man for the magazine. This chart is total bullshit! There is no legitimacy to the chart at all, but they would take a guy, Joe Blow, record him in Nashville, charge him $3,500.00 to record, they would release the record (or what they call "release"), charge him another $2,500.00 to promote it, and low and behold he would show up on that worthless chart in Indie Bullet. The artist would think, "Oh man!" "I'm climbing the charts" "I'm gonna be a big star!" No your not man ! They are conning your ass! They are ripping you off! And to prove my point all you had to do was check your BMI or ASCAP royalties to see what you earned from radio air play and you would have seen 15 cents if you were lucky, most artists never saw one cent, but by the time the artists figured that all out, it was too late, they already got the "Nashville Hustle". And you might say, "OK, that was then, things are different now." I got news for you, they are still doing it today ! The same labels (Different names), the same people are still in it today ripping off artist left and right. The Horror stories coming out of Nashville are unbelievable.

Anyway, Chuck D. and the Nashville crew could not completely control the Texas crew of the Indie Bullet Magazine or Cashbox magazine and they needed a chart to keep the con game going, so they created this magazine called, "Indie Tracker." Indie Tracker is run by a girl, Audrey, who is dating Chuck D. and I might add is controlled by Chuck and his crew. They do the same thing. Phony charts. The whole nine yards. They even go as far as having an, Indie Tracker Award show in Nashville at some shit hole Nashville bar/club. These artists travel in for the award show from all over the globe, thinking it's like a big deal, BUT here's the deal they are gonna give the award to whatever artist has the most financial backing that they know is gonna come with 3 or 4 record releases and they got a controlled chart so they are making the call and it's total bullshit. It's unbelievable. All smoke and mirrors.

Sooner or later Indie Tracker and Indie Bullet start fighting Gangland style. There's a serious feud going on. Now ya got Texas fighting these heavy hitters (Mobsters for a better word) in Nashville. You know who's gonna win that fight right?. Next thing you know, Indie Bullet goes out of business. And Roy Hause disappears. I mean it got to the point where they actually sent a dead fish to Roy Hause in the mail. It was organized crime at it's highest level. Well, before ya know it, Indie Bullet is out. Gone completely, Roy Hause becomes M.I.A. and never heard from again and low and behold, Gary B. moves to Nashville and he joins the Chuck D. crew. And now the con is really on. They've got all the artists from both magazines, they got the Indie Tracker magazine (That they own), they got the charts and they're making money hand over fist. But, always remember, it's all bullshit! It's called vanity labels and fake charts. They do it for the vanity of the artist. And I don't care who you talk to, you will never see one major star that came out of one of those vanity labels charting in one of those fake ass charts. It's just totally unbelievable that they got away with it, and they are still doing it today.

You look at some of these make believe charts today, they can't do it too much in the US so they are pumping them over in Europe.

And they are going to Australia and these small community radio stations that have no power, no clout whatsoever AND they now have internet stations to get reports from, you might see a handful of internet stations that are worthy and actually have a big listener base. !!!. The reality of it all if you want to be the next Garth you need those 50,000 and up watt mainstream AM and FM stations The artist is not making any money on internet stations, and some of them have these playlists and ya see some of these DJ's ( not all of em' now, just some of em' a few of these internet stations are totally legit), but some of these European stations put up their playlist that they have in their show on the internet weekly, and it shows 250 records being played in a show. And today, ya got more phony charts all over the place. One is this girl named Joyce. This is a joke! 200 records on her chart. OK, and of the 200 of em', 50 of the people on that chart are dead! They're fuckin' dead! They're not even recording. They're not even active in the business! It's hilarious, but it keeps going on. And, it goes on today. And that my friend is the Nashville horror story! They are cookie cutter labels, they take your money, they give you fake charts, they give you fake information, and you're broke, and at the end you're right back where you started from but now your a broke ass artist with no place to go. Welcome to the Nashville hustle.

# The Mel McDaniel Last Ride

I've been asked many times to tell the story of how The final album of the legendary Mel McDaniel developed, and how it took place, and finally how it finished. So I'll try to give you the inside scoop of what happened, how it happened, why it happened, and behind the scenes stuff only a few had the privilege to see and hear.

I guess I have to start in 2010. I was going through our business emails, I get at least 100 plus emails a day. Most of them we just delete as we go along, and for some reason I see one that was addressed, Mel McDaniel. I opened it up. I've never met Mel McDaniel. I mean, I know of him. He's a legendary performer. I know of his music. I've listened to it for years, but I've never had the honor of actually meeting him so I was surprised to get an email from him. But in the email he told me he planned to record his final career album, and asked me if I had any songs. Ya know, unrecorded songs that I could send him because he was looking for material for the album. And I agreed to do it, but also in the back of my mind I was asking myself, "Why is a guy that is so legendary in country music packing it all in, and doing a final album?" His fan base is worldwide.

But, anyway, I went through the songs I had written and found one that kinda fit Mel's style. It was called, "Motel 6." And I said, "Let me send him this demo." Anyway, he wrote me back, and he said he liked the song, and he asked me if he could have some time to kick it around and see if it fit him. And I wrote back, and said, "Sure, I'd be honored if you cut it." And then I didn't hear from him I guess for about 2 or 3 weeks. And then I got an email from him, and he asked me if I would be interested in producing his final album. He called the album, "The Last Ride." And at the time we were really jammed up. I mean we had a lot of projects going. I had Doug Kershaw, "The Ragin Cajun" in there to do the Kentucky Headhunters duet of Jessico, Becky Hobbs, Razzy Bailey, Bob Marleys Wailers in there, Jeffrey Steele, Ricky Lynn Gregg, so in short I was jammed up. I wrote Mel back and I said, "Mel, I'd love to do it, but

I just don't have the time." "I can't possibly fit it in." Another week went by, and I got another email from him and it read, "Listen, I want you to do this album." "I'll work around your schedule." "Whenever ya got time, but I want you to do the album." And again, I really couldn't do it. There wasn't enough time available. I wrote him back and said the earliest I could do it would be September or October of 2011 a year later. He wrote back and said, "I'll wait." So I just let it go at that point. We were going back and forth to Nashville at Quad Studios doing our projects and coming back to our studio in Hampton, Virginia The Power Plant and finishing them up.

I guess it was around the end of December or early January of 2010 we were down in Nashville recording and I get a phone call from Mel's manager at the time, Barry, saying, "Mel would like to come meet with you." It was a really difficult session that we had going on at the time, but I said, "Sure, ya know if he just wants to stop in for a while, that would be fine." I had not mentioned to anybody that I was communicating with Mel about the offer to produce the album. So it was a Tuesday or a Wednesday, and we get a call around 12:00 noon that Mel would like to stop in at 2:00pm. We were right in the thick of the session, but I said to everybody listen we're gonna take a break at 2:00, we'll get lunch, and I'm gonna meet with Mel McDaniel. Anyway, to make a long story short, which is gonna be impossible, Mel showed up with his manger Barry, and I was in the control room in Studio "A", and one of my assistants, Janet came in and let me know Mel was here outside in the back lounge. I was doing that project with 2 of my business partners, Bill Reid and Jim Smelgus. And of course I had my studio "A Team" in there. Anyway I went outside to meet Mel, and they had him in the back lounge of Quad in studio "B".

So I went back there, and there he was sitting there. The legendary Mel McDaniel. But, I was shocked to see how much weight he'd lost. He was walking with a cane, but he was still walking, but he was using a cane and was very very frail. I introduced myself. We started talking, we shared "I have a lot of respect for you" and yeah, "I have a lot of respect for you" and "You're legendary "and yeah, "So are you,, legendary" we got all those accolades out of the way and we started to talk.

About halfway through the conversation Barry and Bill Reid went into another room to discuss something. God knows what those 2 were planning? But, me and Mel started to talk. So I asked him, "What's the matter Mel?" "Health wise?" He just told me that he had taken a fall, and had a heart attack, and the doctors were working on him plus he had a carpal tunnel thing going on, but to be honest with you it looked much worst than that. My remark to him was, "Hey Mel, ya know when we get old, everything starts to break." "Including stuff on me." He said, "Ya know Doc, at one time he said I was a 240 pound man." I looked at him, and he looked like in my estimation, he was down to 125 pounds. I mean he had lost a lot of weight.

We kept talking about the industry and about country music. He said he had some material together that he'd like to run by me for the album. I said, "Mel, I 'm not sure if I could do it yet or if I want to do it, they are pushing me pretty hard these days" "Ya know, I would love to do it, it's a great honor, but I don't know." At the end of that sentence he said, "Say Doc, ya know what happened the other day." I said, "What Mel?" He said, "I had to go shopping." He said, "Ya know how embarrassing it is to sit in one of those little scooters and drive around?" I have some knee problems myself so I was walking with a cane so here's these 2 crippled old guys there, ya know. I said, "Hey Mel!" "It don't bother me man." "I just sit in that scooter, and scoot around, blow the horn, and get em out of the way man." "Have fun with it." So he goes, "Yeah, but it's embarrassing." I said, "Nah, it shouldn't be man." "Ya know, when your old, shit starts to break up on ya."

Well right then and there Bill and Barry came back in, and Mel said, "I wanna play you something." I said, "All right." So we got up, and walked to another room in Quad. A smaller studio. You know Mel was walking a little slow and he was hobbling a bit taking baby steps. He was struggling, but he was walking. And we got into this room, and we sat down and he said, "I'm gonna play you this song that I never let anyone hear." It was just a demo with Mel playing the guitar. The song was called, "Damn the loser." He had written it about his first and now ex wife. I listened to the song, and the song was pretty cool. I said, "I can do something with that." "I can fix that and make it work." He said, "I really want to do this record Doc"," I said, "Mel, I gotta find the time to get it done, I'll let ya know." He said, "Doc, this album is important to me." "I have to do this album." I said, "OK but again I'm jammed up Mel." We started to talk again about other stuff and I said, "Listen, ya wanna come in the control room, and meet Bobby Bradley before you leave." So he said, "Yea." Then I walked out, and he kept talking to Bill and Barry. I said to Bobby Bradley, my engineer and has been for the past 19 years. Bobby is originally from Bradley's Barn, The home of Owen Bradley. They called Owen,"The Architect of Country Music" and he was legendary in country music and recorded every major country star in his day at the helm.

I walked into the control room and said, "Bobby, I got Mel McDaniel outside, and I wanna bring him in to meet everybody. And he said, "Really?" "I recorded Mel 25 years ago." I said, "Are you serious?" "Where?" He said, "At the barn." "When Owen was still alive." I said, "Really?" He said, "Yeah man." "He did two songs." "They were off the hook." He also said, "He never released the songs." "One was called, "Sugar Mountain" and the other was called, "Roll you own." I said, "Really." So anyway I went out in the hall where Mel was waiting, and I said, ' Come on Mel." "Let's meet everybody." Immediately Bobby and him recognized each other. So now Mel has a real comfort zone because here's a guy that was with Mel at his hay day at Bradley's Barn with the legendary Owen Bradley. And we're all sitting around talking, and we all took a couple promo pictures together. Gotta get a photo opt, met all the players and everything else, and looked at the studio. And Mel was in the chair behind the board, and I said to Mel, "Mel I'll let you know on this thing as soon as I can." "I just need to think about it a little bit." He said, "OK." He said, "I'll do it whenever you want me to do it." "But, I want you to do it." I said, "OK." So when he left, I looked at Bobby and I said, "He wants us to do this final album, The Last Ride." I said, "I don't think I wanna do it." "I don't feel comfortable with it." "He's in pretty bad shape." Ya know, and I don't know if he can even sing anymore he's so damn weak?" "He's having enough problems walking let alone singing." Bobby said, "Yeah, but Doc." (and I'll never forget this). Bobby looked at me and said, "He's still got that fire in his eyes." He's still got that fire." I will always remember that moment, and I said, "OK."

So we finished that session we were working on, and I went back to Virginia and was working on what I had just recorded in Nashville and I thought about it and thought about it and thought about it and I said, "Ah, maybe I can do this?" "Maybe we can squeeze this in some place?" Now it's early January, and Mel is writing me all the time about this thing. So finally I said, "OK Mel." "Let's get together, and see if we can get this thing started?" So I called Bobby, and I said," OK, we're gonna do this album on Mel McDaniel." And we started to line up all the players. I really thought about doing the album holding nothing back and I said to Bobby and my conductor Dale Herr, "If we're gonna do this thing, let's do it unbelievably," "All right? let's pull all the plugs out and bring in the greatest players in the world!" So we brought In: Craig Krampf (This is my full bore "A Team" and these guys have been with me anywhere from 15 to 19 years). Craig is famous for probably playing drums on every single Alabama album that every hit the charts. He also won the Academy Award with Flash Dance, he was also a writer on "Oh Sherry" for Journey, he did the Kim Carnes records, "Betty Davis Eyes." And the list goes on and on and on... He's a legendary drummer. Then, I wanted to get a little different with Mel because he always had this in his music, this little rock edge, this fun "in you face" thing with' "Stand Up", "Blue Jeans" and that stuff.

So I brought in a bass player, Garry Tallent, who has been with us for a long, long time. Garry's from Bruce Springsteen's East Street Band and a member of The Rock and Roll Hall Of Fame. And I'll just run through the rest of the players. There was a ton of them that day. I had Sandy Pippen on piano who's a legendary Nashville session player. The arrangements and guitar was Dale Herr (One of the main guys on the "A" Team), another legendary player on steel guitar was Pat Severs, and Pat is from The Pirates of the Mississippi and also steel guitar player for Charlie Rich and worked on the Grand Ole Opry for years. So he had a lot of different edge going to him. Ah, we had Brett Lind, who is Bobby's assistant on the thing, and he ran the Pro Tools and the computer. And of course, Bobby Bradley from Bradley's Barn on the board. Then we brought in Jim Horn who is a legendary sax player and horn player. Jim has played with each of the Beatles separately. Plus he was with Kenny Chesney for years. His credits just go on and on and on and is known in the industry as "The Most Recorded Sax Player in the History of the Music Business".

I know I'm gonna forget people on this session cause there was so many of them. The girl back ground singers that you hear are the Deb Thomas Singers from Nashville. Like I said, this is my studio "A Team", and these are the guys I use all the time. They know what I want before I tell them so we're a tight knit family. We got the team together, and it was difficult cause guys like Garry had to fly in from Montana. So it was a serious undertaking.

So we met with Mel again, and when I met with him, his health had deteriorated big time. And I said to Bobby, "Listen, if we're gonna do this thing, we gotta do it quick!" "All right, cause he's not doing well." We scheduled that session two weeks from that meeting. And I said, "OK, we're gonna fly this bitch, and we're gonna do this." So everybody was on edge. We got into the session, and I said, "I want Mel there for tracking." Normally, the singer isn't there. We do the tracks and then we bring the singer in and he sings his parts over the recorded tracks. I wanted Mel there in the beginning because I wanted a comfort zone with him because I knew mentally he had a way he wanted these songs to go and what he wanted to get that across with my people and of course I was gonna rearrange everything and change it around a lot, so I wanted him to be comfortable with the tracks.

So Mel came in, and when he came in, his

health had really gone down hill. And I was really concerned if he was gonna be able to do this? He was sitting at the board with me, and I remember we started to do one of his songs, and he said to me in a real low labored voice, (it was very difficult for him to talk). He said, "Doc, it's too fast." So I slowed it down a little bit. We played it again. And he said, "it's still too fast." I called out to the guys, and said, "Listen guys." "Ah, where ya at on this thing?" And I remember Craig saying," 110." And that's the speed of beats that you get to set the tempo. I said, "Drop it down to 105. I dropped it down to 105 and Mel said, "It's still too fast." So I'm saying, "Wait a minute." "The demo is like at 130." I said, "All right, drop it down to 100." We dropped it down again and Mel said it was still too fast. And at that point I'm saying, "OK, we've got a problem here." "Because this thing is like 30 points off of the demo." And I said, "Mel, you're sure man?" "This thing is crawling." So he looked at me, and he goes, "Oh man, I'm looking at the wrong song!" Now, I know we've got a problem. because he was so, what would I say, medicated that it was difficult for him to concentrate. I said, "No problem Mel, I'll fix it", and we got it rolling again.

And then he said to me, "I wanna Johnny Cash feel on one of the songs." I believe it was, Roll Your Own?" I forget right now. So I said, "OK a Johnny Cash feel." Now we already had our players in place, but I went to Bill Reid, and said, "Listen, get me David Roe on the phone." And those of you who don't know who David Roe is, he was Johnny Cash's bass player for the last 15 years of John's life. And I said, "See if we can get David Roe in here to play on this thing with my guys to give it that Johnny Cash feel. And they made the phone call, and sure enough, David said I'll be there. And Dave came in and nailed it big time as only he could do it. So when you hear the slap bass, that legendary Johnny Cash slap bass in the song, that's David Roe doing what only he can do. We got all the tracks done, and then we needed one day to mix down the tracks to get em ready for the vocal parts. Mel went back home to rest, and then we were gonna start the vocals.

Now there was only 48 hours before we had seen Mel, and when he came back 48 hours later to do the vocals, his health was just...it was terrible! I mean the poor guy couldn't even walk anymore. And for some reason he would not take no for an answer. He wanted to do this album. So I said, "OK, let's get it on," I put him in the vocal booth, and when you listen to the album, it' s actually in the order that we did the album so you'll hear the first song he's sounding pretty bright and full of energy. And as the album goes on, his health deteriorated so bad, and it was difficult at the end. But anyway, we got him in the booth, and he went in and started to sing and I really gotta give the credit to Bobby Bradley here because Bobby was all over it and just taking his time and making sure everything was tight, and if it wasn't tight for Mel he would correct it and make it work, and we started recording. The first day Mel put in about, I guess seven or eight hours in that booth? It was at one point, the pain was so bad, his manager ( I guess I'm not supposed to tell this?) but ya know, I gotta tell the story the way it is. The manager came up to me and said, "Listen, I'm gonna go to the hospital, and get him some medication." The medication was Morphine because he was in such pain. Well, once he took the medication, he was good for another three or four hours. But he wouldn't quit. Ya know, I just said, "Mel, let's call it quits." "Let's spread this over five or six days." He just wouldn't stop. He had to do this album.

Well to make a long story short, and I know I've been saying that all along, but the story keeps getting longer. Comes the final day with Mel, and he's really, really, really bad. I mean he can't even pick up his head. He's got oxygen tubes in his nose to help him breath, an intravenous running in his arm with morphine running in him, and I can still remember him sitting in that vocal booth on the stool with all the damn tubes running in him. I mean he's a tough guy. He really is. He's a tough son-of-a-bitch! And he's sitting in there with the tubes and a jug of water, and a cigarette in his God damn hand. I said, "Melvin? Are you fuckin crazy, ya got oxygen in there, you'll blow us all the fuck up", Mel said "Na it aint lit I just wanna hold it"" Anyway, he's struggling through these songs, and finally it got to the song "The Last Ride" and three days before we did the album, I sat down, and I wrote the song, "The Last Ride" based on his career. And I said, "Hey, I got the title song of your album." And I gave it to him so he didn't have any chance to rehearse it or anything. He just read it, and listened to my demo, and he loved the song, and he said we're gonna do it. So that became the title song. So anyway, we got to the song, "The Last Ride", and he was just in no condition to continue on, and it was hurting me to see what he was doing to himself. I walked in and I said, "Mel, listen, ya don't have to do this man." "Ya don't have to do this." "Let's pull the plug on this thing." "We'll come back." "We don't have to do this song, "The Last Ride" and "The Gun Fighter" and I think the other one was, "Sugar Mountain." I said, "We don't have to do these songs." "We got enough songs to go with it." "Ya know." And he looked at me, and he said, "Doc, I'm dying!" "I have to do this album!" And I just stood there, and I was just lost for words and I turned around and looked at Bobby at the control room and I said, "Bobby", let's roll this mother fucker". And Old Mel just gave me a big ass smile And we started to cut "The Last Ride."

I remember saying to him, "Mel, ya don't have to sing it like I sang it on the demo," "Talk it." "It's the story of your life man!" "Just talk it." "Tell the story." We finally got "The Last Ride" done, and I said, "OK listen, I gotta get outta here because it was really starting to upset me, how he was beating himself up. And I asked Bill to take over for a little bit so I could take a break and clear my head out. I went to a place called Noshville to get some coffee and a sandwich. And as soon as I got in there, I get a phone call on my cell phone, and it was either Bobby Bradley or Bill? I don't remember who it was? They said, "Doc, ya gotta come back to the studio." "Mel needs you to sing these last two songs so he can get the phrasing right on it." I said, "All right." I turned around, went back to the studio, knocked out the two songs, and again told Mel, "Ya don't have to sing em man." "Don't sing em like I 'm singing em." "Talk em." "They're message songs." "The whole album is about you." You can even talk it Mel." "That's all it is."

The last day the man came in at 10:00 in the morning, and didn't leave till nine o'clock that night. He never left the booth. The only break in the whole thing was when Becky Hobbs had come by to talk to me about another recording session, and she was a huge fan of Mel McDaniel. And she said, "Can I meet him?" And I said, "Becky, he's in pretty bad shape." She said, "OK, but I'd like to meet him if I could?" And we opened up the vocal booth. By the way Mel didn't want any cameras in the studio and we always had video cameras in there, and he wanted all the cameras off him all the time. He didn't want his fans to see the condition he was in so no one was allowed to take pictures. There was no video cameras running, and I was a little hesitant to bring a visitor in. Especially, Becky Hobbs. But I went in, and I said, "Mel, Becky Hobbs is out here, and wants to meet you." And he goes, "Really!" I said, "Yeah." He said, "Bring her in." I said, "OK." "Hey, a good lookin' blonde, that will cure you real quick!" Ha! Mel McDaniel might have been sick, but he was still Mel McDaniel! So we brought Becky in, and I remember them meeting in the vocal booth, and she says, "Can I get a picture with you?" And Becky sat on Mel's lap, and we've run the picture a couple times. If you look real close, you can see the oxygen tubes in Mel's nose when it was being taken. But, that kinda brightened his day a little bit, and gave him a little bit of energy. Thanks Becky! And he knocked out the last song "Damn The Loser" he finished at 9:00 that night.

We, Me & Bobby worked on the album all the rest of that night...because Bobby was breaking it down word for word, line for line . It was that difficult, and then put it all together to make it sound right. And at 9:00 o' clock in the morning we are still working on this thing. We figured we had three days of work in Nashville on the album, and bring it back to Hampton, Virginia to the Power Plant and finish it up there another four or five days. We get a call at 9:00 that morning while we are still in the studio. They took Mel to the hospital. He's in I.C.U. in critical condition. And that's when we found out that Mel had terminal lung cancer, and it was not operable. And he wasn't gonna be around too much longer. I didn't know that. No one in the studio knew it. Mel knew it, but he would not quit. He wanted to do this album. So what you hear in that album, is definitely Mel McDaniel's last ride! This man moved people during that record session like no other human being could. He's a man's man. No doubt about it! And he lived his life to the end, and he got his message out to his fans and friends and everybody else the only way he knew how to do it. Through his music. Me & Bobby rushed and did a final mix on the song "Damn The Loser" he wrote for his first wife that was so important for him to record on this album and we rushed to the hospital with a CD player. When we got there Mel was laying in that hospital bed and just a short time away from doing his last ride. I leaned over him in bed with a portable CD player and said, "We finished the loser Mel" I hit the play button and the song started to play. At the end of the song he looked at me with those sad eyes and said "Your A Fuckin Magician". I will never forget that moment. So Mel, you were the best my man and together, We made Magic and We got er done Melvin!!!!

# My Last Words on the Subject
## (Well Maybe)

Well, that about wraps this book up. At least for now anyway. Those are just some of the events and stories that happened in my life related to the music industry and the entertainment industry. And believe me, there were thousands and thousands more stories and events that I never got to tell in this book. But, maybe if I live long enough, and all the law suits are settled from this book, I'll write another book, and mention some of the other stories and events that I missed?

But for now I think that gives you a rough idea of how I became who I am, and rest assure I am what I am, and it was just a small part of what happened along the way. You all know me as Doc Holiday, and of course by now you realize that's not my real name, but that's the name I've used for the past 50 years.

I've been pretty successful in the music industry or should I say "I got pretty damn lucky", but as you now know by reading this book, there's been a lot of ups and downs and a lot of scary moments along with some Great Moments that I would not trade for anything. But, I wouldn't have it any other way.

My daughter Carmela asked me once again the other day, she said, "Dad if you had to do all over again, what would you change?" My answer was still the same and very simple, "I wouldn't change a damn thing." "I'd do it all the same way." "With one exception." I would remove the booze and drugs." Other than that, it would all go down exactly the same way it did.

I take pride in my work, and I will till they put me in the ground, which lately could be any damn moment. Everytime I did a record, every time I enter a project, I gave it 110 percent and still do. It's personal to me, That artist that I'm producing is actually me at one time in my life with that same dreams I had and I never took that lightly. Thankfully, I'm still able to do that, Give it all I got.

My health is failing now, and it's about time

that I left something down in print so people who are fans of mine will know what took place. Ya know through it all, I was loved and respected by the people I wanted to be loved and respected by. I was hated and criticized by people I never gave a fuck about and still don't give a shit about them. So all in all, I think it all kinda worked out pretty good for me.

So before I leave, I'm gonna leave you with a quote that just kept pushing me through my journey. DREAMS LAST FOREVER,,, WE JUST RUN OUT OF TIME!!! I'll see you next time I hope. If not, IT'S BEEN ONE HELL OF A RIDE, AND FOR WHAT'S IT'S WORTH, I'M GONNA KEEP RIDEIN' THIS BITCH UNTIL THE WHEELS FALL OFF!!!!

Doc Holiday

Oh, one more thing about Country Music to those young artists out there trying to get into the business, Just because you have a twang in your voice and your recording has a hot guitar lick in the recording, That don't make it Country Music! Trying to do Rock Pop and labeling it country music, just because you drive a pick up truck and wear a baseball cap backwards and sing with a southern accent, Don't make it Country Music!

IT'S REAL SIMPLE SPORT FANS, "COUNTRY MUSIC IS THREE CHORDS AND THE TRUTH" Remember that.

www.ingramcontent.com/pod-product-compliance
Lightning Source LLC
Chambersburg PA
CBHW072045090426
42733CB00032B/2260

* 9 7 8 0 5 7 8 1 8 8 0 9 6 *